SASKATOON

SASKATOON

A HISTORY IN PHOTOGRAPHS

Jeff O'Brien, Ruth W. Millar, & William P. Delainey

COTEAU BOOKS

Editor for the press, Geoffrey Ursell.
Edited by Roberta Coulter.

Cover images – Top: "Broadway Bridge, Saskatoon," © Pro-stock Images, Saskatoon.
Bottom: "Downtown Saskatoon, c.1912," courtesy Saskatoon Public Library.

Cover and book design by Duncan Campbell.
Printed and bound in Canada by Houghton Boston, Saskatoon.

Library and Archives Canada Cataloguing in Publication

O'Brien, Jeff, 1962-
Saskatoon : a history in photographs / Jeff O'Brien, Ruth Millar, & William P. Delainey.

Includes index. ISBN 1-55050-336-7

1. Saskatoon (Sask.)—History—Pictorial works. 2. Saskatoon (Sask.)—History. I. Delainey, William P., 1942- II. Millar, Ruth III. Title.

FC3547.37.027 2006 971.24'25 C2006-900184-7

1 2 3 4 5 6 7 8 9 10

COTEAU BOOKS
2517 Victoria Avenue
Regina, Saskatchewan
Canada, S4P 0T2

AVAILABLE IN CANADA AND THE US FROM
Fitzhenry & Whiteside
195 Allstate Parkway
Niagara Falls, NY, USA 14305-1386

The publisher gratefully acknowledges the financial support of its publishing program by: the Saskatchewan Arts Board; the Canada Council for the Arts; the Government of Canada through the Book Publishing Industry Development Program (BPIDP), and the support of this publication by the City of Regina Arts Commission; Saskatoon Citizens Centennial Committee, and the Saskatchewan Cultural Industries Development Fund of Saskatchewan Culture Youth and Recreation.

Saskatchewan Arts Board · Canada Council for the Arts / Conseil des Arts du Canada · Canada · Regina City of Regina · Saskatoon Our time to shine 100 2006 · Culture, Youth and Recreation

This book is dedicated to the memory of William A. S. Sarjeant. During the thirty-some years he lived in this community, he promoted and documented Saskatoon's history as editor of the *Saskatoon History Review* and helped preserve the city's architectural heritage through his work with the Saskatoon Heritage Society and the Municipal Heritage Advisory Committee. He also co-authored a number of local history publications, including *Saskatoon: A Century in Pictures* (1982), which commemorated the founding of this settlement a hundred years earlier. At the time of his death in 2002, Dr. Sarjeant was anticipating his involvement in this updated companion volume to celebrate the 2006 centennial of Saskatoon's incorporation as a city.

SASKATOON

GREAT WEST SADDLERY CO.
THE GREAT WEST SADDLERY CO. LIMITED

WESTERN BOOK
Simpson's
1952 OLYMPICS

PERIOD

Foreword

This compilation of historic photographs celebrates the centennial of Saskatoon's incorporation as a city in 1906. A companion volume to *Saskatoon: A Century in Pictures* by William P. Delainey, William A. S. Sarjeant, and John Duerkop (Western Producer Prairie Books), which was published in 1982 to commemorate the hundredth anniversary of the founding of this community, this book includes many never before published images found in the growing collections of the Saskatchewan Archives Board and the Local History Room at the Saskatoon Public Library. The photographs selected are accompanied by a brief overview of the decade they represent in Saskatoon's history to give readers a better understanding and appreciation of this community.

A host of institutions, publications, organizations, and individuals were consulted to bring this project to fruition. We are especially grateful to the Saskatoon Public Library's Local History Room, the Saskatoon office of the Saskatchewan Archives Board (SAB), the Saskatoon City Archives, the *StarPhoenix,* the University of Saskatchewan Archives, and the Meewasin Valley Authority (MVA). This book could not have been produced without the unstinting aid provided by the people who work at these institutions: Cheryl Brown, Ron Jaremko, George Kovalenko, Mary Ellen Schnitzler, and Kathy Snider at the Local History Room; Nadine Charabin at the SAB; Steve Gibb and Brian Johnsrude at the *StarPhoenix;* Cheryl Avery and Patrick Hayes at the University of Saskatchewan; and Nola Stein at the MVA. We would also like to acknowledge the contributions of a number of individuals who provided valuable information and photographs, including: Larry Bertell, Rusty Chartier, John Duerkop, Dick Epp, Dennis Fisher, Les Howard, Mike Jenkins, Blaine Knoll, Al Ledingham, Traycee Martens, Noreen Matthews, Allan Morton, Greg Pender, Ross Pinder, Doug Porteous, Glen Reeve, Peggy Sarjeant, Harold Sokyrka, Barb Sprigings, Dale Yellowlees, and Wayne Zuk.

We would like to thank the Saskatoon Citizens' Centennial Committee and the Mayor's Office for their support of this project. We would also like to acknowledge all the advice and assistance we received from our publisher, Coteau Books, and its staff.

Finally, our most profound thanks to our families and friends. While writing is generally a solitary pursuit, no writer truly works in isolation. For this reason we would like to acknowledge the debt we owe to the special people in our lives: to Bill's spouse, Deb England, for her support, advice, and technical assistance; to Jeff's wife, Kathy, for her unstinting co-operation and endless patience; and to all of Ruth's family, for their support and encouragement.

Bill Delainey, Ruth Millar, Jeff O'Brien

Preface

1882-1906

Saskatoon was founded in 1882 on the eastern bank of the South Saskatchewan River, in the area we now call Nutana. It was an experiment in social engineering based on the idea that most of society's ills could be traced to the effects of alcohol. If alcohol was the cause, the reasoning went, then abstinence was the cure. With ideals held high, the Temperance Colonization Society of Toronto set out to mould the virgin territories of the west into a prohibitionist utopia (and to turn a profit in the process).

Alas, the temperance colony failed both ideologically and financially. But it did produce a viable settlement, which through a combination of good luck, geography, foresight, and hard work would ultimately become the city we know today.

The Society had been granted a large parcel of land along both sides of the South Saskatchewan River between Clarke's Crossing and the present-day Whitecap First Nation. In the spring of 1882 a party under John Lake travelled west to survey the area and choose a townsite for the new colony. At only one point were both river banks low enough to allow for an easy crossing. Here they

---

Opposite page: An aerial view of Saskatoon, ca. 1928. The Broadway area of Nutana is in the foreground. The 1928 Town Planning Board recommended the construction of another bridge, which would connect Broadway to 19th Street at 3rd Avenue on the west side, and renewal of the area including Chinatown along 19th Street west of the Traffic Bridge. *Photo LH 4243 courtesy SPL – LHR* stopped, camping on the higher east bank in the present day Idylwyld neighbourhood in northwest Nutana. This would be Saskatoon.

The first settlers arrived the following spring. They travelled by rail as far as Moose Jaw and then hauled their goods and equipment overland some 250 kilometres to the new colony. Until the first railway came through on its way to Prince Albert in 1890, this was the only way to Saskatoon: a long, hard slog through what was often described as a trackless and barren desert. Yet they persevered.

Isolation, drought, frost, and poor crops made the next few years very hard. While the 1885 Northwest Resistance was an economic bonanza for some merchants, sensationalized reports of it in the newspapers back east deterred many potential settlers. The Wild West, it appeared, might be just a little too wild. As well, the shallow, meandering South Saskatchewan River turned out to be unsuitable for any kind of regular commercial navigation. No riverboats and no railways meant that there was no economical way to bring goods in or ship agricultural products out. The settlement survived, but just barely.

The arrival of the Qu'Appelle, Long Lake and Saskatchewan Railway (QLLS) in 1890 was not the ticket to prosperity many had hoped, but it probably saved the colony from extinction. It was also responsible for the first settlement on the west side of the river in what is now downtown Saskatoon. The railway station was built there and commercial and residential establishments soon followed. Very quickly, the west-side settlement became the dominant one, even to the point of taking the name Saskatoon for itself. The original colony renamed itself Nutana, apparently a scrambled inversion of Saskatoon.

The temperance colony failed both ideologically and financially. But it did produce a viable settlement, which would ultimately become the city we know today.

The two adjacent communities grew very slowly over the next decade. While the trickle of settlers into the Canadian prairies had become a veritable torrent after 1896, settlement tended to concentrate first in those areas most easily accessible from the existing rail lines. But as this land filled up, the Saskatoon area began to seem a great deal less remote. By 1903, things had begun to improve. The arrival of the Barr Colonists that spring (on the way to their own version of utopia near present-day Lloydminster) provided a very significant boost to the Saskatoon economy. That year Saskatoon was incorporated as a town and the settlement of Riversdale was established. By 1905, a growing population in all three centres, the need to provide an increasingly complex administrative framework and infrastructure, and the fierce competition to be named capital of the new province of Saskatchewan led them to amalgamate. On May 26, 1906, Saskatoon's city charter was given royal assent in the provincial legislature.

This is where our story begins.

RDON & SPARLING — BUTCHERS

Chapter One
1906-1909

When Saskatoon was formally incorporated as a city on May 26, 1906, the city fathers – casting an optimistic eye toward the future – spread their arms wide. Bounded by Clarence Avenue on the east and Avenue P on the west, and extending from Taylor Street north to 33rd, the new city encompassed fully fifteen square kilometres of rolling prairie, most of it uninhabited. Nearly all of Saskatoon's 4,500 residents lived clustered together within a few blocks of the river.

Within three years, three major railways were routed through Saskatoon, firmly establishing it as the distribution and transshipment point for the surrounding districts and making it the most important transportation and commercial centre between Winnipeg and Edmonton. Commercial, wholesale, and industrial development began to take shape along the rail lines that cut through the city north of the Canadian Northern yards downtown, along the Goose Lake and the Canadian Pacific lines on the west side, and south of the river along the old QLLS line where the Idylwyld Freeway now runs.

Opposite page: Settlers and livestock dealers on 2nd Avenue South, ca. 1907. The downtown business area was expanding from its core, the railway station at 1st Avenue and 20th Street East. The Empire Hotel (now the Capri Place apartments) at 2nd Avenue and 20th Street East is in the right background. *Photo LH 1101 courtesy SPL – LHR*

The town of Saskatoon in the spring of 1906, viewed from the east side of the river, just before it was incorporated as a city on May 26 after amalgamating with the adjacent villages of Nutana and Riversdale. The Empire Hotel (left middle) and King Edward School (right middle) were landmarks. *Photo C 555/2/5-12f courtesy U of S Archives*

But while they were joined by legislation, the three communities continued to be separated by geography. The river and the railways had brought them together, but they also served to keep them apart. Until the problem was dealt with, Saskatoon would be a city in name only.

Recognizing this, Nutana held out for the promise of a road bridge to add to the existing railway bridge across the river before it would agree to amalgamation. The ferry service was irregular and generally unreliable. If Nutana was to be a full partner in the new city, there would have to be a better way for people and goods to move back and forth. All parties agreed that a bridge was necessary, and the provincial government promised to pay for it. Construction began in 1906, and the Traffic Bridge officially opened on October 10, 1907.

Cut off from the rest of the city by the rail yards separating 1st Avenue and Avenue A, Riversdale was in a similar position to Nutana. In 1909 the railway agreed to allow subways to be dug beneath the lines south of 19th and at 23rd Streets (in addition to the level crossing at 24th Street) and a footbridge was built over top of them near

Local dignitaries and citizens greet Governor General Earl Grey at the Qu'Appelle, Long Lake and Saskatchewan (QLLS) railway station (then at 1st Avenue and 20th Street East) in August 1906. *Photo LH 920 courtesy SPL – LHR*

20th Street. It was a not a perfect solution, and Riversdale continued to exist in semi-isolation until the downtown rail yards were removed in the 1960s.

In 1906, Saskatoon's city council authorized the installation of sanitary sewers and water supply systems, as well as an electrical power network. Construction also began in 1908 on a new fire hall on 23rd Street and 3rd Avenue. For the time being, civic offices were located two blocks south, at the corner of 3rd Avenue and 21st Street on the site of the latter-day Eaton's Department Store (now the offices of the Saskatoon Public School Board).

Saskatoon's first permanent buildings went up during this period, notably the Flanagan (now the Senator) Hotel, the Chubb Block, a number of office buildings, and the J.F. Cairns store at 2nd Avenue and 21st Street (which was destroyed by fire in 1912 and rebuilt across from the King George Hotel on 23rd Street, where the Hudson's Bay Department Store was later built). St. Paul's Hospital was established in 1907 at its present location during one of the city's regular typhoid epidemics. A new City Hospital was built two years later.

James R. Wilson in his office at the Saskatoon Flour Milling plant (later purchased by Quaker Oats). As mayor in 1907, he gave his personal guarantee on a loan to complete the joint water pumping station and power plant (now part of the water treatment plant) on Avenue H South. *Photo LH 621 courtesy SPL – LHR*

The growing population prompted the building of a number of new schools and expansion of others. King Edward School on 23rd Street between 3rd and 4th Avenues doubled in size. Alexandra School was built on 20th Street West, and temporary structures were built to house students in the new Ashworth Holmes and Caswell Hill neighbourhoods. Construction began on a larger, grander Victoria School on Broadway at 11th Street (the third on that site), and in 1909 the city's first high school, the Saskatoon Collegiate Institute (now Nutana Collegiate), opened its doors.

The construction of a provincial district court house and a land titles office on 21st Street East established the city as a regional administrative

The official opening of the Traffic Bridge on October 6, 1907, viewed from the home of former Mayor Clinkskill on Spadina Crescent East. The school with the tower (centre background) was a prominent landmark as well as cultural centre in Nutana at the time. Directly to its right is the "little stone school," dating from the temperance colony era. It was moved to the university campus in 1911. *Photo PH 89-158 by Ralph Dill, courtesy* SPL – LHR

centre as well. In 1907, local leaders persuaded the board of governors of the newly established University of Saskatchewan to locate its campus in Saskatoon over competing bids from Regina, Prince Albert, and Moose Jaw. The expansive, attractive site they offered on the high east river bank was a deciding factor. In the years to come, the university would help support Saskatoon's economy while at the same time playing a major role in its social and cultural life.

The city's annual fair had originally been held at the Louise Grounds in Nutana (now home to Nutana Collegiate) before moving to what is now Kinsmen Park in 1905. In 1909 it relocated to its present site on city-owned land at the south end of Lorne Avenue. Now the Exhibition was free to construct permanent structures and to expand as necessary. At about the same time, the forerunner to the Saskatoon Golf and Country Club was established just south of the new Exhibition grounds and facilities for other organized recreational activities – curling, hockey, baseball, and football – began to be constructed.

Communications were revolutionized when the first automatic telephone system in Canada was installed in Saskatoon in 1908. It connected a reported 180 customers and was operated under city charter by a local businessman, John C. Drinkle. In 1906, the city acquired a second newspaper, the *Capital* (later the *Star)*, which began operation in direct competition with the established *Phoenix*.

Ethnically, Saskatoon remained largely an English reserve amidst the multicultural mix of people then settling in the area. This was especially true on the Nutana side of the river, which remained primarily upscale and residential. The local chapter of the Women's Christian Temperance Union (WCTU), for example, formed in Nutana in 1906, had its greatest following there, despite (or perhaps because of) the fact that all the bars and liquor outlets were west of the river. Ironically, the city's first brewery sprouted right on the fringes of Idylwyld, long one of the city's ritziest neighbourhoods.

What cultural diversity Saskatoon could boast in those days was concentrated largely on the west side. It was here – and particularly in bustling, brawling Riversdale – that the most affordable housing and broadest range of employment opportunities were to be found.

There were downsides as well. The winter of 1906–1907 was one of the harshest in the city's history, with temperatures of -50 degrees Fahrenheit being recorded. The extreme weather brought rail service between Saskatoon and the outside world nearly to a halt, compounding the effects of a coal shortage caused by labour strikes in neighbouring Alberta. The long winter also made for a poor crop in 1907, which naturally had an effect on Saskatoon. More important was a global economic crisis that began in the spring of that year. The civic administration – mortgaged to the hilt to pay for Saskatoon's new public utilities – was suddenly faced with bankruptcy, a fate it only avoided because of the willingness of Mayor James R. Wilson and other members of the local business community to borrow against their personal credit to support it.

By the end of 1909, the foundations of the new city had been laid. While each of the original three settlements retained something of its original flavour – gracious Nutana, hard-work-

In May 1908, the construction crew posed in front of the nearly completed Canadian Pacific Railway (CPR) bridge at what is now 33rd Street. It connected the company's trunk line from the east to its new depot in Saskatoon. With the completion of the Grand Trunk bridge and the takeover of the existing Qu'Appelle, Long Lake and Saskatchewan railway line by the Canadian Northern Railway, Saskatoon became a hub of the three major Canadian railways. *Photo LH 3384 courtesy SPL – LHR*

The first train arrived at the newly completed CPR station at 24th Street and Avenue A (now Idylwyld Drive) on June 15, 1908. The CPR division yards were located at Sutherland, about five kilometres east on the other side of the river. *Photo LH 3760 by City Studio, courtesy SPL – LHR*

Despite the complications of 1907-1908 it had been a period of steady growth. The population had doubled in three years and the future looked bright. The next few years, however, were to bring such sweeping changes as to beggar the imagination of even the most extravagantly optimistic. Nothing that the people of Saskatoon had yet experienced could have prepared them for the wild roller-coaster ride that was coming.

ing Riversdale, and commercial Saskatoon – they now formed an integrated social and administrative unit. The city's economic role in the region had been firmly established, and the form of its townscape had been cast. Civic leaders were confident that the city's existing fiscal and administrative structures, and its system of public utilities, would be sufficient to meet the demands of future growth and expansion.

Although not without their problems, the preceding three years had generally been good for the new city.

The wreck of the steamship *City of Medicine Hat* against a pier of the Traffic Bridge in June 1908, signalled the end of attempts to use the river for commercial transport. James Clinkskill's house (centre background) was one of the first large residences to be built along the river bank. *Photo LH 1834 by City Studio, courtesy SPL – LHR*

Nurse Sisley's private hospital at 308 6th Avenue North in 1907. The city took over its operation that year, replacing it with a larger frame structure on Queen Street at the north end of City Park (now Kinsmen Park). *Photo LH 1326 courtesy* SPL – LHR

The last annual fair in City Park (now Kinsmen Park) was held in 1908. It was moved to the present exhibition grounds location the following year. The celebration of Saskatoon's incorporation as a city had been held in front of this grandstand, in conjunction with the July 1 opening of the 1906 fair. *Photo LH 909 by Peter McKenzie, courtesy* SPL – LHR

The seven teams of horses Billy Silverwood (fourth from left) reportedly sold for $5,025 in 1909. He raised horses and sold bottled water from a spring on the ranch he owned north of the city (now Silverwood Heights). The livery stable behind, at 135 2nd Avenue South, would become the site of the Bank of Nova Scotia (until 1980) and the entrance to the Capitol Theatre. *Photo PH 87-116 by Ralph Dill, courtesy* SPL – LHR

An Aboriginal couple journey south on 2nd Avenue in 1909. They are passing the intersection with 20th Street, where sewer and water lines were being installed. *Photo LH 435 courtesy* SPL – LHR

Guests pose for a photo during a party held at a residence on Broadway, ca. 1906. Temperance remained strong among the residents of Nutana, but their social gatherings were reportedly as lively as in other areas of the city. *Photo LH 357 courtesy* SPL – LHR

Looking southwest over Nutana from the water tower at 11th Street near Broadway, ca. 1909. Nutana's wide streets, like those in downtown Saskatoon, are a legacy of its temperance colony origins. The stone Garrison house (since demolished) at Broadway and 10th Street also dated from the pre-railway era. The Grand Trunk railway bridge (centre background), completed in 1908, is still part of the CNR line on the southern margin of the city. *Photo LH 3217-1 by Dicker and Dunsford, courtesy* SPL – LHR

Grace Fletcher, an early temperance colonist, successful businesswoman, and suffragette, relaxes at her Nutana home with a young neighbour, Rachel Stephenson, ca. 1906. Fletcher was a prominent member of the Nutana Methodist Church at Eastlake and 10th Street East and provided a large endowment for the new building constructed on the same site in 1910 (now Grace-Westminster United Church). *Photo LH 499 courtesy* SPL – LHR

A carpenter, Joe Provost (right) and his assistant, Mr. Pema, pause with their horse-drawn cart of paint cans and equipment at Avenue C and 20th Street West in Riversdale, ca. 1908. *Photo LH 156 courtesy* SPL – LHR

Alexandra School (at Avenue D and 20th Street West), constructed in 1906, was the first school in Riversdale. Here, students line up to enter the school, which had a new four-room addition and flush toilets. The school had just been connected to the sewer and water system in 1908, ending the need for outhouses on the grounds. In 1985, Alexandra School and Princess School (which was built on the same block in 1911) were replaced by the present Princess Alexandra School. *Photo LH 789 courtesy* SPL – LHR

Local citizens pull a carriage carrying their local MLA, members of the University of Saskatchewan board of governors, and the mayor, from the Canadian Northern railway station on April 8, 1909. Governors Bell and Clinkskill had just returned from Regina with news that Saskatoon had been chosen as the location of the new provincial university. A torchlight parade followed that evening. *Photo LH 1982 by Ralph Dill, courtesy SPL – LHR*

After a new firehall was built at 23rd Street East in 1908, the town office and firehall on 3rd Avenue between 21st and 22nd Street East served as both city hall and police station until the city could afford better facilities. The new brick Saskatoon District Court House is visible on the far right. *Photo LH 990 by Ralph Dill, courtesy SPL – LHR*

The Labour Day parade passes the Drinkle Building at 21st Street and 2nd Avenue North in the fall of 1909. Constructed in 1907, it was the first of a number of commercial blocks erected in Saskatoon by John C. Drinkle, a local developer. The inaugural classes of the University of Saskatchewan were held in its top storey while the first buildings were being completed on campus. The Drinkle Building was destroyed by fire in 1925. The present MacMillan Building was built on the site soon after. *Photo LH 4770-b by Peter McKenzie, courtesy SPL – LHR*

ERN
DIMENSIONS

Chapter Two
1910-1913

The period 1910-1913 was a time of unparalleled economic and physical growth for Saskatoon. Not before nor since has the city changed so utterly in such a short time.

The population jumped from around 10,000 in 1909 to a staggering 28,000 by the end of 1912. The total assessed property value quadrupled to $36 million. Otherwise reasonably sober individuals were confidently predicting a city of 50,000 by 1915 and 100,000 by 1920. The Church Union Committee forecast a population of 65,000 by 1921, and no less a personage than the president of the university predicted that Saskatchewan as a whole would have 2,000,000 inhabitants by 1931.

Imposing commercial buildings echoing the architectural styles of Winnipeg and Chicago sprang up in Saskatoon's downtown core. Stately homes and beautiful cathedrals lined the river banks, and the first buildings were going up on the new university campus. Money was easy, optimism was everywhere, and real estate was king.

Opposite page: Local promotion and entrepreneurship contributed to the phenomenal growth of Saskatoon during the boom period. Here, Mayor Hopkins (left) stands with board of trade commissioner F. Maclure Sclanders and a young woman next to the Saskatoon Board of Trade office on 1st Avenue, just south of the Canadian Northern Railway station in 1909. The garden in which they stand showed visitors the area's great agricultural potential. *Photo LH 5391 courtesy SPL – LHR*

Workers take a break from digging ditches for sewer and water mains at 23rd Street East and Spadina Crescent in 1910. The city's capital budget and civic debt increased significantly that year so that it could provide the utilities and services necessary for Saskatoon to reach its projected potential. *Photo LH 1814 courtesy SPL – LHR*

Saskatoon was still a British town. The 1911 census showed that 80 per cent of its citizens traced their ancestry back to the British Isles. Various European and Slavic ethnic groups trailed far behind. The census did not record any persons of Native ancestry living in Saskatoon, but the city's business directories of the day did show an increasing number of Jewish and Chinese shops and restaurants, and there is evidence of an active Italian community.

The people of the city were proud of the gothic-style greystone collegiate buildings that were being built on the new University of Saskatchewan campus, located on the river bank northeast of the original temperance colony townsite limits. An elegant new concrete bridge was to be built across the river at 25th Street, linking the university with downtown. No less wonderful was the city's first public transit system, which opened on January 1, 1913. That first year, the streetcars of the Saskatoon Municipal Railway carried almost 3.5 million passengers over a distance of almost one million kilometres. By the end of the year, it had been extended all the way out to Sutherland.

The new 1,200-seat theatre addition to the Empire Hotel on 20th Street East became the most popular venue for touring performers during this period. The number of pool halls, bars, and smaller theatres increased each year. "Flickers" – early silent movies – began showing regularly in addition to live entertainment. By May of 1913, the city could boast eight movie theatres with a total of 4,200 seats. The annual show at the exhibition grounds, with accompanying midway, grandstand performers, and horse races, was a popular attraction each summer. In winter, the local senior hockey club competed in the amateur Southern Saskatchewan Hockey Association. In 1912 the Saskatoon Westerners challenged Port Arthur in a Stanley Cup playoff.

Looking northwest from the corner of Spadina Crescent and 1st Avenue South in 1911. Work crews are excavating a traffic subway under the Canadian Northern Railway tracks to connect downtown with Riversdale. It was filled in when the 19th Street subway was built in 1931. In 1912, a second subway was excavated under the tracks at 23rd Street on the northern margin of the rail yards. *Photo LH 1821 courtesy SPL – LHR*

The 20th Street East end of the pedestrian walkway over the Canadian Northern Railway yards, ca. 1911. Built in 1910, it was a major foot-traffic corridor between Riversdale and downtown until it was torn down in 1963, just prior to the downtown rail yards being removed. *Photo LH 3243 by Benjamin Skewis, courtesy SPL – LHR*

By 1914, a semi-professional baseball team played at the new Cairns Field just north of the CPR yards on Avenue A near 26th Street. Finally, Saskatonians seeking to wet their whistles could choose among fourteen bars and three liquor outlets.

Several new public elementary schools were built during this period, all in a distinctive castlelike architectural style. A Catholic school system was organized in 1913 and operated in St. Paul's Church basement until permanent quarters were completed. The Saskatoon Public Library opened the same year. The YMCA and YWCA both opened in grand new brick buildings downtown, and former mayor James Clinkskill's grand house on Spadina Crescent at 19th Street (on the site of the present-day River Landing development) was purchased by the federal Department of Militia to be converted into an armoury.

Saskatoon owed its sudden good fortune to the flood of immigrants pouring into the area in search of homesteads. Its central location on the rail lines connecting east to west made it the major service and distribution point for a huge rural hinterland. The Saskatoon Board of Trade, the Industrial League, and numerous entrepreneurs touted the city's advantages far and wide. By the end of 1912, more than 100 square kilometres of rolling prairie in and around Saskatoon had been surveyed into streets and lots and offered for sale. That anyone would have invested a penny in such properties seems incredible. After all, it took decades for the city to expand to fill even that area within its own city limits, let alone the distant subdivisions that lay beyond. But invest they did. This was Saskatoon, the "Fastest Growing City in the British Empire," and fortunes were begging to be made.

Few stories illustrate the triumph and tragedy of the boom as well as Factoria, the proposed industrial park north of Saskatoon in what is now Silverwood. It was the brainchild of Chicago developer Robert E. Glass and Billy Silverwood, a local horse breeder and bottled water magnate, who hoped to convince companies to locate there, and then to sell residential lots to the workers and their families. A number of businesses did set up shop in Factoria and a hotel was even built, but city council balked at the expense of running a power line that far out, and the project stalled. When the boom finally went bust, so did the dream of Factoria.

View from the pedestrian walkway at 20th Street of the eight-storey Canada Building as it neared completion in 1912. It is directly across the street from the new Canadian Northern Railway station at 1st Avenue and 21st Street East. Built by local developer Allan Bowerman, the Canada Building was advertised as the highest building west of Winnipeg. It provided the best bird's-eye view of the city around it for years to come. *Photo LH 2478 courtesy* SPL – LHR

Other planned subdivisions were even less successful. Developments with strange names like Swastika Park, Utopia, and Megantic Park never existed at all save as lines on a map in the provincial registry office.

Nonetheless, Saskatoon was growing fast. The expanding city required an expanding infrastructure to support it. In 1910, civic officials embarked upon an ambitious program of public improvements, adding significantly to the sewer and water-main system laid down in the previous four years, building sixty-five kilometres of paved sidewalk and, by 1912, over six kilometres of paved roads. The water pumping plant at 11th Street West and Avenue H was enlarged and a water treatment facility added. In 1911, the city built a new coal-fired power plant near the river bank on Avenue A to replace the old one next to the pumping station. Finally, in 1912, a new city hall opened in what had formerly been King Edward School, on 23rd Street between 3rd and 4th Avenues.

That all of this building was debt-funded was completely by the by. Saskatoon was booming, and in the fall of 1912 there was no end in sight. City council was in the process of adding some two million dollars to its debt for further public works in 1913 when – just as in 1907 – the boom went suddenly and disastrously bust.

There were a number of causes, almost all of which were related to the global economy and well beyond the power of any purely local initiative to overcome. Credit dried up. The banks in Saskatoon – which had been only too happy to lend money to even the most improbable of investors – suddenly refused credit to anyone, and began calling in existing loans.

Saskatoon's overheated real estate market collapsed. Construction stopped, literally overnight. Houses were left unfinished. Buildings planned for ten stories were hastily completed at five. Entire streets of open excavations were left to show where workers simply packed up their tools and left. All planned extensions to the city's utilities were cancelled and the number of civic staff was halved.

The view from the roof of the Canada Building of development to the west, ca. 1913, including the Canadian Northern Railway yards, Riversdale, and beyond. In the centre background is the Quaker Oats plant (formerly the Saskatoon Milling Co.). To its right is the new St. Paul's Hospital, nearing completion on Pleasant Hill at Avenue P and 20th Street West. *Photo LH 3816 courtesy* SPL – LHR

A few of the land speculators who had fuelled the Saskatoon dream made a great deal of money. Most did not, and some lost everything. The common folk – the waitresses and clerks who had taken a gamble in the market at 5 per cent down and the rest in monthly installments – fared even worse as Saskatoon's economy followed that of the western world into dramatic decline.

But the full extent of the calamity was not yet apparent, and the unswerving

The Grey Nuns established St. Paul's Hospital in Dr. Willoughby's former residence (left) on Pleasant Hill in 1907, to provide care for those suffering from a typhoid epidemic sweeping the city at the time. In 1913, they moved the hospital into a large brick structure (right) constructed adjacent to the original building. *Photo LH 1068 courtesy SPL – LHR*

optimism of the boom years was not the kind of thing that could be derailed by a series of mere financial disasters. People continued to hope that it was all nothing more than a little pot hole on the road to prosperity. Some welcomed it, suggesting that anything that put an end to the ruinous speculation in land could not help but prove beneficial in the long run. Development even began on new industrial parks in the north and west, construction started on the University Bridge, and there was a general feeling that the downturn in the economy was a temporary thing.

This optimism was not completely unrealistic. Saskatoon had, after all, survived a similar economic crisis only a few years previously and gone on to do such incredible things as would hardly seem imaginable. But this time the recession was to prove deeper and longer than expected, and it ended not with an economic recovery but with an even greater disaster: the First World War.

John East Iron Works, at 121 Avenue C North in Riversdale, originated in 1910 as a family business, producing manhole covers and other castings for the city's sewer and water system. It was to expand on that site and remained the main iron and steel supplier for Saskatoon and district until it closed in 1975. *Photo LH 3979 courtesy SPL – LHR*

Looking northwest from the roof of the Canada Building, ca. 1913, over the warehouse area between the Canadian Northern Railway and CPR yards and beyond. Caswell School (centre background) is surrounded by an expanding residential area. The stately residence of John C. Drinkle (right background) stands on the large block of land he owned east of Avenue A to 33rd Street. Cairns baseball field is nearing completion just north of the CPR yards (right middle). *Photo LH 1534A courtesy SPL – LHR*

Saskatoon firemen pose in front of the Fire Department's first automotive fire engine in Fire Hall No. 1 at 23rd Street and 4th Avenue North, ca. 1911. To the left, harnesses hang ready to be dropped on a team of horses that would pull the fire wagon (behind the fire engine). *Photo LH 444 courtesy SPL – LHR*

Looking northeast, ca. 1913. The former King Edward School, which served as city hall and police station after 1910, is on the far left. Across 23rd Street (left centre) is the No. 1 Fire Hall (where the Main Public Library is presently located). In the centre background is the new King Edward School (now the site of the YWCA) at the south end of City Park (now Kinsmen Park) on 25th Street. Behind it is the new City Hospital on Queen Street at the north end of the park. *Photo PH 88-634G by Benjamin Skewis, courtesy SPL – LHR*

A doll drill performed by young students as part of a concert to raise money for a bell for the new King Edward School, ca. 1912. *Photo LH 160 courtesy SPL – LHR*

In 1911, a new municipally owned City Hospital was built next to the old frame one (left) on Queen Street at the north end of City Park, taking up part of the Saskatoon Golf Club's course (it later became the Saskatoon Golf and Country Club, located south of the exhibition grounds on Lorne Avenue). The original building was used as an annex for a number of years before it was demolished to make room for an addition to the main building. *Photo LH 1836 courtesy* SPL – LHR

Students in the chemistry laboratory in the basement of the College Building on the University campus during the 1912-13 term. *Photo A-1653 courtesy U of S Archives*

In 1911, the existing power house at Avenue H South and 11th Street was converted into a water pumping and treatment plant. The Parks Board, which planted thousands of trees in parks and on boulevards throughout the city, operated the city gardens, located just to the north. Across the river are some of the first large houses (right background) built in the Idylwyld subdivision of Nutana, the only area in the city where private lots back directly on the river. *Photo LH 1824 courtesy* SPL – LHR

Looking southeast from the roof of the Canada Building, ca. 1913. A major addition, including a theatre, has been made to the Empire Hotel (right middle). The Auditorium Roller Rink (and hockey arena in winter) on Spadina Crescent (left middle) burned in 1914. On the Nutana side is the No. 3 Fire Hall and water tower next to the new Victoria School (built in 1908) at Broadway (left background). Saskatoon Collegiate (now Nutana Collegiate) is at the top of the "short hill" at the south end of the Traffic Bridge. *Photo PH 96-200 courtesy* SPL – LHR

The College Building – shown here under construction in the winter of 1911 – was the first of the gothic-style greystone collegiate buildings completed on the university campus. It was completed in 1912, at a cost of $297,000. Structural problems plagued it from the beginning, however, and it was closed for safety reasons in 1997. It reopened in 2005 after an extensive renovation and rehabilitation project costing more than $20 million. *Photo A-24 courtesy U of S Archives*

Some of the prestigious residences backing on the river in the Idylwyld area of Nutana, ca. 1912. The house with the tall Greek-style columns at 307 Saskatchewan Crescent West was built in 1910, by then-mayor William Hopkins, a hardware merchant and land developer. *Photo 88-643 courtesy* SPL – LHR

On March 4, 1912, "The Kipling", a sleeper car on a passenger train leaving from the Canadian Northern Railway station downtown, crashed to the ice below when the northern span of the bridge collapsed. A number of passengers were injured but fortunately no one died. In the background is the new Saskatoon Power House (later part of the now-demolished A. L. Cole plant), located close to the centre of the city at 19th Street West and Avenue A in Riversdale. *Photo LH 2003 courtesy* SPL – LHR

By 1913, commercial development was extending to 3rd Avenue. The MacMillan building (now the Avenue Building, left middle) and the Connaught and Glengarry blocks, which were nearing completion (right middle), blocked the view from the cupola on top of the Flanagan (now Senator) Hotel. The cupola was removed ca. 1944. This photo was taken from the top of the seven-storey Ross Block (demolished in 1986) on 3rd Avenue between 21st and 22nd streets. *Photo PH 88-634A by Benjamin Skewis, courtesy* SPL – LHR

Residential development such as that shown here along 5th Avenue North ca. 1912 was taking place around the city centre. The rows of elms that shade these areas today are a legacy of the Parks Board. *Photo SL-LH-94 by Ralph Dill, courtesy* SPL – LHR

Crews lay streetcar tracks along 20th Street West from Avenue A. These tracks were connected via the 23rd Street subway to the lines already installed along 2nd Avenue downtown. The Saskatoon Municipal Railway began operation on January 1, 1913. *Photo LH 3635 courtesy* SPL – LHR

A view of 21st Street East, ca. 1913, from the Canadian Northern Railway station to Spadina Crescent on the river bank (where the Bessborough would later be located). One of the early St. Louis "puddle jumper" street railway cars is passing through the intersection with 2nd Avenue. The Bijou Theatre (left foreground) had originally been James Clinkskill's store. The building has since been demolished, but the word "Clinkskill" is still embedded in the concrete sidewalk at that location. *Photo LH 4060 courtesy* SPL – LHR

The new King George Hotel (left) and the large J. F. Cairns department store (later the Hudson's Bay Company store) at the intersection of 23rd Street and 2nd Avenue, ca. 1913. Here the streetcar tracks turned to serve the West Side via the 23rd Street subway (centre background). *Photo PH 90-74-33 courtesy* SPL – LHR

A crowd gathers in front of Fawcett's Hardware in the Kempthorne Block at 157 2nd Avenue North to see the inning-by-inning results of a 1913 baseball playoff game in Moose Jaw, being posted by a CPR telegraph operator. The Saskatoon Quakers played in the semi-professional Western Canadian Baseball League between 1910 and 1914. *Photo PH 98-38-21 courtesy* SPL – LHR

Employees of the Arctic Ice Co. haul ice blocks cut from the river, ca. 1913, for storage in its plant (in the background), then just south of the water plant on Avenue H. Arctic Ice was the major supplier for iceboxes in the homes and stores of Saskatoon until refrigerators became widely available in the 1950s. *Photo LH 1126 courtesy* SPL – LHR

In 1913, two members of the Saskatoon Country Club (now the Saskatoon Golf and Country Club) examine the layout of their new course on land leased from the city next to the exhibition grounds. The construction of the new City Hospital had required the club to vacate its original site in City Park (now Kinsmen Park). Bill Kinnear was the golf pro at the club from 1910 to 1945. He designed the club's first nine-hole course in 1910. It was later known as the "pansy nine," now the site of the Marquis Downs racetrack. *Photo LH 5265 by Helen Schrader, courtesy* SPL – LHR

By 1913, a racetrack and a number of permanent buildings had been constructed on the present exhibition grounds, then some distance south of the city. *Photo LH 2687 by Hillyard and Free, courtesy* SPL – LHR

Looking east on 6th Street (now 110th Street) toward Central Avenue in Sutherland, ca. 1911. Sutherland grew up around the CPR divisional rail yards east of Saskatoon. The Saskatoon Public Board ran the Sutherland School (centre background). Despite Sutherland's close association with Saskatoon (including a connecting street railway line), its residents chose to incorporate as a town in 1912, rather than become part of Saskatoon. The two finally amalgamated on January 1, 1956. *Photo LH 3963 courtesy* SPL – LHR

The brick plant of the Northern Brick Tile & Supply Co., ca. 1913, located north of Saskatoon in what is now Silverwood. This was one of the few buildings actually constructed in Factoria, a proposed industrial subdivision north of Saskatoon. Boosters' plans for the area also included houses and a hotel in addition to commercial facilities. Unable to convince the city to run a power line out that far, they saw their dreams finally dashed by the recession that ended Saskatoon's pre-First World War real estate boom. *Photo PH 87-112 by Ralph Dill, courtesy* SPL – LHR

Looking west along 21st Street East to the Canadian Northern Railway station at 1st Avenue on a busy summer morning, ca. 1912. The balcony on the Flanagan (now Senator) Hotel in the left foreground was used as a platform for public announcements – such as for the official announcement in 1909, that the university would be located in Saskatoon – as well as an outdoor lounge for hotel guests. *Photo LH 562-1 courtesy* SPL – LHR

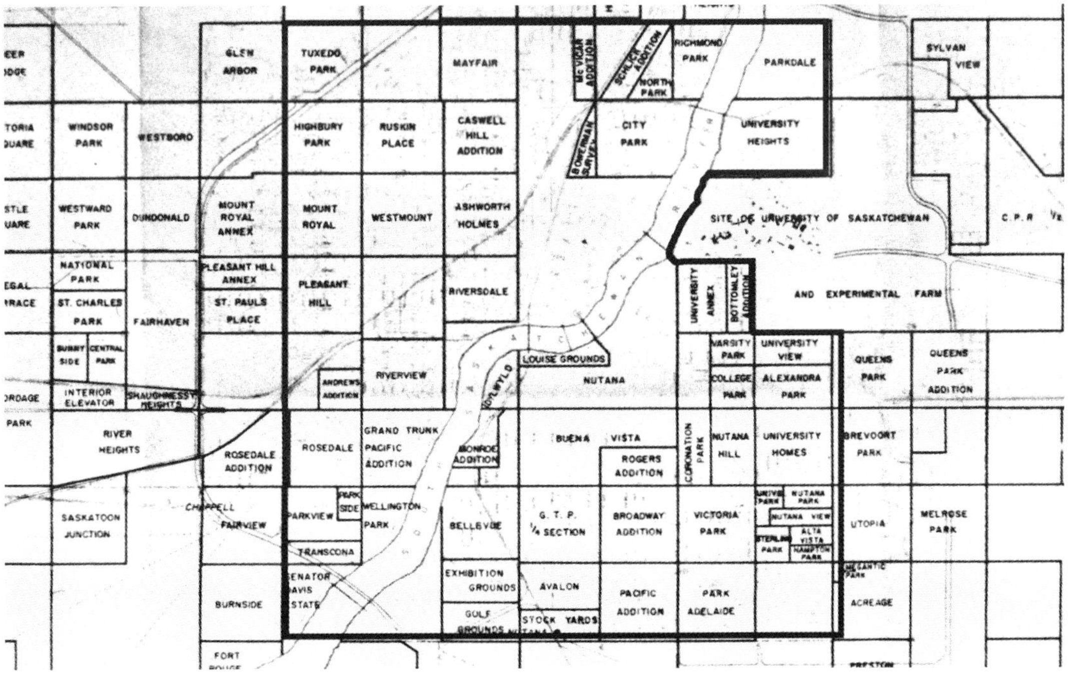

Registered subdivisions within Saskatoon's corporate limits and surrounding district as of 1913, are superimposed on a 1968 map with Circle Drive shown to provide perspective. *Map courtesy City of Saskatoon, Building and Planning Department, 1968*

CANADA'S GREATEST SALE
The MONTREAL BANKRUPT STOCK Co.
212 22nd ST.
216 22nd ST. East
BUTLER BYERS

Chapter Three

1914-1919

The bust that followed Saskatoon's amazing real estate boom must have seemed like a bad dream to those who lived through it. But it was nothing compared to the nightmare that was in store, both for Saskatoon and for the rest of the western world. Political tensions among the rival nations of Europe had been simmering for years and finally, in the summer of 1914, they boiled over. Suddenly the British Empire was at war, and Saskatoon with it. The first volunteers left the city by mid-August, less than two weeks after Great Britain's entry into the war. By the end of 1918, more than 10,000 men from the Saskatoon area had enlisted.

Even the most cheerful optimist now had to agree that the city's boom was finally finished. But the situation – already bad – got rapidly worse.

By December of 1914, 2,500 Saskatonians – one in ten – were on relief. The year that followed was even worse, ranking as the most dismal year in Saskatoon's economic history until the Great Depression of the 1930s. All construction, including public works projects, had come to a complete halt with the beginning

---

Opposite page: Although Saskatoon's boosters were reluctant to accept it at the time, the economic boom had ended. By the end of 1914, bankruptcy brokerages such as this one in the Royal Block on 22nd Street East were doing an active business, while many real estate development and construction-supply companies were closing their doors. Butler-Byers Ltd. (right) was one of the earliest real estate and insurance firms in Saskatoon. *Photo LH 5263 by Helen Schrader, courtesy SPL – LHR*

A postcard, inscribed by a Saskatoon fan, of the first game played in the new Cairns Field on May 14, 1914. The field, located on Avenue A (now Idylwyld Drive) just north of the CPR tracks, was named in honour of local merchant J. F. Cairns, who was largely responsible for its construction. *Photo PH 89-80 courtesy SPL – LHR*

of the war. Construction on the University Bridge stalled when the contractor went broke, and the provincial government was forced to step in to finish it. The war did help to stabilize Saskatoon's economy (largely due to the increased demand for agricultural products), but it also ended the city's dreams of developing the necessary industrial base to become more than strictly a regional centre.

The city's population dropped during this period, from an estimated high of 28,000 in 1912 to 21,000 in the federal census of 1916. The population rose again over the next few years but would not surpass its pre-war levels until the mid-1930s.

As a result of the Great Bust of 1913, thousands of properties were forfeited to the city for non-payment of taxes. In some cases, the owners simply walked away when the real estate market collapsed. Others held on grimly, sometimes for years, paying their taxes faithfully in the generally vain hope that some day their property might be worth something. Although this was to prove beneficial in the long term, for the present it only made the city's financial problems worse, as not only were there no new buyers for the lots but now they were not generating any tax revenue either.

At first, everyone thought it would be a short war. "Home by Christmas" was the common refrain. But the months turned into years, and even in Saskatoon there was no escaping the war. The newspaper headlines spoke of nothing else, and the lists of the dead, wounded, and missing seemed to grow longer every day. Letters from men serving overseas arrived opened and resealed with an "Opened by Censor" stamp on them, and soldiers had to sign a statement "on their honour" that their letters home spoke only of private family matters. But even these precautions could not completely hide the horrors of trench warfare from the people at home. Those left behind contributed to the war effort in any way they could. Women increasingly took up men's positions in the work force (although not to the extent that was to occur during the Second World War).

Saskatonians bought half a million dollars worth of Victory Bonds, and charitable organizations like the Patriotic Fund, the Red Cross, and the International Order of the Daughters of the Empire (IODE) supported both the men overseas and their families at home.

In 1916, Saskatchewan women won the right to vote in provincial elections. In a possibly related development, prohibition struck Saskatoon that same year, as first the bars and then the government liquor stores were closed. Saskatoon voters (including the newly enfranchised women) showed their temperance-colony roots and voted 10 to 1 in favour of prohibition. It was the highest proportion of wet versus dry votes in the country. Liquor could still be imported from out of province, however, and Saskatoon did not truly go dry until the federal government declared total prohibition in the spring of 1918.

In 1914, Canada's entry into the war had been received in Saskatoon with bands and parades. The celebrations lasted for a week. On November 11, 1918, a world traumatized by four years of war celebrated the coming of peace. The armistice was announced just after midnight. In Saskatoon there were parades and bonfires lasting through the night, and the celebrations went on into early morning.

Although the people of Saskatoon rejoiced to see their men return home from the bloody battlefields of France, an uninvited guest rode the train cars back with them. The Spanish flu epidemic of 1918 would kill more people worldwide than the war had. More than 5,000 died in Saskatchewan, 2,500 in November alone. In Saskatoon, thousands were infected, with 224 recorded deaths in October and November of 1918. It tore through the population, striking young and old, rich and poor. But in contrast to other diseases, which tended to prey mostly upon the very young and the very old, its preferred victim seemed to adults in

Construction in the downtown ended quite suddenly in 1914. Some buildings then under construction, intended for eight or more stories, were capped off at one or two stories. Others, not yet started, were cancelled, leaving scattered empty lots. In 1912, people thought the Standard Trust building (centre background) at 3rd Avenue and 22nd Street would soon be surrounded by buildings as high or higher. It continued to tower above those around it until it was demolished in 1976 to make way for the Sturdy Stone Centre. *Photo PH 90-74-28 by Hillyard and Free, courtesy* SPL – LHR

Construction of the University Bridge, begun in 1913, was delayed when the contractor went bankrupt. It was finally completed in 1916 under the direct control of the newly formed provincial Department of Highways. The spire of St. John's Anglican Cathedral (left background) was the tallest structure in the city at that time. *Photo LH 3588 courtesy SPL – LHR*

the prime of life. More than 60 per cent of all influenza deaths in Saskatchewan were people aged twenty-five to forty.

Medically, it was a mystery. There was no cure, and even the precise means of transmission were not understood. "I opened a window and in flew Enza" went one saying, and perhaps that was as good an explanation as any. At its height, schools and churches were closed and all public meetings were banned. People were advised to wear gauze masks to protect against airborne infection, and any number of quack remedies were advertised as cures or preventatives. But the only real solution was to wait it out and hope for the best. Thankfully it was short-lived. Although the epidemic continued to claim lives until as late as 1920, the worst was over by December 1918.

Saskatoon breathed a sigh of collective relief. But the years immediately after the war also offered much political and economic turmoil. While Saskatoon had benefited somewhat from high agricultural prices during the war, the increased cost of living had not been matched by increases in wages. When agricultural prices collapsed at war's end, a recession hit the city. Construction materials and other goods continued to be in short supply. Housing shortages and unemployment were a constant source of misery, with more and more men returning from the fight to find inadequate jobs, inadequate wages, and inflated prices. Political and labour unrest spread across the country, and leaders here and elsewhere feared the spread of Bolshevism and other radical political ideologies among the restless working classes, returned soldiers, and farmers. The Winnipeg General Strike, which paralyzed that city for several weeks in the summer of 1919, was felt here as well, when Saskatoon's unionized workers went out in support of the general strike.

By the end of 1919, as the decade that had begun so well but ended so poorly finally drew to a close, the people of Saskatoon could only wonder what new surprises awaited them in the decade about to begin.

A contract to supply expansion plates for the University Bridge provided an important source of revenue for the John East Iron Works (located at Avenue C and 22nd Street West) during the recession that followed the end of Saskatoon's pre-war real estate boom. *Photo LH 3990 courtesy* SPL – LHR

The end of a long summer day: boys pose on the river bank within the municipal bathing enclosure, ca. 1915. *Photo LH 5247 by Helen Schrader, courtesy* SPL – LHR

The municipal bathing pond in the river directly below the water plant on Avenue H South. This log-boomed enclosure was constructed by the city in 1914, to provide citizens with a safe designated swimming area. Local boat owners later built a small marina just north of this pond to moor their rowboats and sailboats in the summer. *Photo 93-166-17 by Charmbury's Studio, courtesy* SPL – LHR

Although the city hall employees in this 1915 photograph managed to keep their jobs, the city had cut its annual budget and civic staff by half in 1914, following the start of the First World War. At the time, office and clerical work was primarily a men's domain. *Photo LH 4738 courtesy* SPL – LHR

Public utilities and services in residential areas close to the city centre, such as along Lansdowne Avenue in Nutana, shown here, ca. 1915, were maintained during the recession. *Photo LH 3774 courtesy* SPL – LHR

In 1914, with the possibility of war looming in Europe, young men from the Saskatoon area began enlisting for military duty. Here, recruits march south on 2nd Avenue, likely to the armouries (next to the Clinkskill house, which served as the officers' mess) on Spadina Crescent. *Photo 2002-141-25 courtesy* SPL – LHR

Some houses that had been built in unserviced areas were moved onto lots connected to sewer and water lines. Here linemen cut the power lines so this house could be moved eastward along 33rd Street West near Avenue A (now Idylwyld Drive), ca. 1916. *Photo LH 4774 by Norris M. Trickey, courtesy* SPL – LHR

On the morning of August 24, 1914, a crowd follows soldiers of the 105th Fusiliers and 26th Light Horse regiments as they march west on 23rd Street East toward the subway and the CPR station, where they would be carried east, first to training camps in Canada and ultimately to see active service overseas as part of the 1st Canadian Division. *Photo PH 2002-141-21 courtesy* SPL – LHR

The 105th Fusiliers and the 26th Light Horse regiments trained in Saskatoon at the armouries (then on Spadina Crescent East), and at the exhibition grounds. Here, in two overlapping photos, they are shown in a joint military-church parade on the grounds behind city hall. The 3rd Avenue Methodist Church is in the right background. *Photo LH 5407 courtesy* SPL – LHR

Bob Frank and George Morley prepare to set off on an epic trek to New York by motorcycle. There they planned to ship for England to enlist directly in the British Army. They arrived in New York on August 2, a journey of 5,500 kilometres in seven weeks. Although both survived the war, they never returned to Saskatoon. *Photo PH 95-92-1 by Ralph Dill, courtesy* SPL – LHR

The cast of a local production to raise money for the war effort, on stage at the Empire Theatre, ca. 1916. Attached to the Empire Hotel on 20th Street East, the theatre was then the main venue for public performances in the city. *Photo LH 4065 courtesy* SPL – LHR

In 1917, the T. Eaton Co. established a catalogue warehouse in Saskatoon on Avenue D North, next to the CPR tracks. It occupied the former Stamco Mattress Company building (left), plus the adjacent two-tiered structure (constructed in 1917) until after 1929, when the large Eaton's department store was completed on 3rd Avenue North. Federated Co-operatives owned and occupied the building on the left from 1944 until it was torn down in the 1960s. The two-tiered building on the right has had a number of occupants, including the Canadian Royal Ordnance Corps during the Second World War. It is now being converted into residential condominiums. *Photo LH 37 courtesy SPL – LHR*

Despite the war, ordinary activities occupied most Saskatonians. Here three young coeds on the University campus pose for a photo while on their way to a tennis match, ca. 1915. *Photo E.VII.5, Jean Murray fonds, courtesy U of S Archives*

Looking east at the main building at the Forest Nursery Station, just south of Sutherland in the summer of 1916. It was established by the Federal Department of the Interior in 1913, to produce seedlings for prairie farm shelterbelts. The large building (left) is the superintendent's residence (now a City of Saskatoon municipal heritage property). *Photo LH 5135A courtesy SPL – LHR*

The funeral procession for Captain R. Bateman, October 13, 1918, proceeds north on 3rd Avenue past the MacMillan Building (now the Avenue Building) at 21st Street East. He was a professor at the University of Saskatchewan before enlisting in the Western University Battalion and was killed in action in France on September 3, 1918. Captain Bateman was one of the few Saskatonians killed overseas whose body was brought home for burial. However, many others are remembered by the elms and plaques along Next-of-Kin Memorial Avenue at Woodlawn Cemetery. *Photo PH 89 260 by Steele's Studio, courtesy SPL – LHR*

The funeral procession for William Hamilton, a university student, winds its way through the campus in November 1918. He contracted the Spanish flu while working as a volunteer nurse in the temporary hospital the city had set up in Emmanuel Hall. Over two hundred residents died during the epidemic that swept Saskatoon that fall. The residence of the Dean of Agriculture (now the Faculty Club) is on the left. Saskatchewan Hall is on the right. Nutana is visible in the background. *Photo A 5709 courtesy U of S Archives*

Chapter Four

1920-1929

The years immediately following the end of the First World War were difficult ones in Saskatoon both socially and economically, but by 1926, after thirteen years of just barely hanging on, things in Saskatoon were finally beginning to look up.

The city's population grew from 25,000 in 1921 to 31,000 in 1926 and a whopping 43,000 by 1931. As raw materials became available again following wartime shortages, construction began anew. The value of building permits issued by the city – always a good indicator of economic health – hovered around the one million dollar mark each year during the first half of the decade but climbed rapidly thereafter, peaking at nearly six million in 1929.

Many much-needed public buildings went up in Saskatoon during this time. The Saskatoon Sanatorium – a provincial tuberculosis hospital – was built at the south end of Avenue K, and both St. Paul's and City hospitals were expanded. Elementary, high school, and university enrolments doubled. The Saskatoon Normal School (teachers' college) was built, as was the School for the Deaf and ten

Opposite page: Automobiles follow a streetcar from the Traffic Bridge up the Long Hill to Broadway Avenue in Nutana in the early 1920s. The University Bridge is in the distance. *Photo LH 3892 courtesy* SPL – LHR

In 1920, Great War veteran Stan McClelland (centre) and two associates established a commercial air service on the western outskirts of the city using a Curtiss JN-4 biplane. *Photo PH 96-80-11 courtesy SPL – LHR*

new elementary and high schools. A new public library was built across from city hall, and a new branch library was established on the west side of the city. Construction began on a police station in 1929 – previously the police department had been located in the basement of city hall – as well as on a new federal office building. Public restrooms – the "Comfort Station" – were built in Market Square at 21st Street and Avenue A, where Fire Hall No. 1 now stands on Idylwyld Drive. The Children's Aid Society opened a new children's home near the railway tracks at 6th Street and Kilburn Avenue (the site of the present-day Kilburn Hall facility for young offenders).

Although there were some notable additions to Saskatoon's industrial base (particularly in the automotive and home appliance industries) during this time, most of the increased industrial capacity of the city continued to be agriculturally based. Robin Hood Flour bought the old boom-era Northland Milling Company flour mill in Factoria, north of Saskatoon, and later built a new mill on 33rd Street. The Union Stockyards opened on 11th Street West, and an automobile factory even operated out that way very briefly.

The introduction of national chain department stores irrevocably changed the retail industry in the city. Eaton's opened on the corner of 21st Street and 3rd Avenue in a brand-new building, and the Hudson's Bay Company moved into the J. F. Cairns store at 23rd Street and 2nd Avenue.

Saskatoon's Chinatown – concentrated along 19th Street downtown – flourished during the 1920s. Chinese laundries, grocery stores, and restaurants thrived. Housing conditions, however, were quite poor, and the Chinese community was treated with suspicion by authorities. Suspected opium dens were the targets of police raids, and allegations of involvement in the white slave trade were not uncommon. To its credit, the City of Saskatoon refused to enforce a 1919 provincial law which tried to discourage the hiring of white women by Chinese businesses. At the end of the 1920s, however, Chinatown was bulldozed – a casualty of Saskatoon's first exercise in urban renewal – to make way for the new Saskatoon Technical Collegiate and a legion hall.

Public health made great strides forward during this decade. The water supply – which had for many years caused annual typhoid epidemics – was made suddenly safe by the building of a chlorination plant in 1924. Vaccinations for diphtheria and scarlet fever began in the early 1920s, and pasteurization of milk was made compulsory in 1923. Outdoor privies continued to flourish, however, despite the efforts of the city's medical health officer. By 1924 there were still more than 3,000 outhouses in Saskatoon. More than half the houses in the city had them, many on streets with existing sewer and water lines. For many, particularly in the city's poorer neighbourhoods, the cost of installing plumbing was simply more than they could afford. Better economic times in the last half of the decade helped reduce the number of "unmodern houses" in Saskatoon substantially, but the Great Depression of

The Pike Lake Water Carnival and regatta, August 10, 1921. Pike Lake became a popular recreational site for Saskatonians after 1912, when the Saskatoon Auto Club (founded by J. F. Cairns) built a dock and a domed pavilion on its shore. *Photo LH 5423C by Ralph Dill, courtesy SPL – LHR*

the 1930s was to reverse the trend, and in 1932 the medical health officer would report that outdoor privies were as much a menace as they had been when the battle began, ten years earlier.

Most residential development during this time was along existing streets, particularly in the sparsely populated fringe areas north of Queen Street and southeast of Nutana. Gradually, new houses began to fill in the many gaps left behind when the pre-war real estate boom went bust. Although construction rates remained low during the first part of the decade, things picked up by the mid-1920s. In 1926 the number of houses built nearly doubled the previous year's rates and housing starts continued to climb, peaking in 1928.

Saskatoon's green spaces had been woefully neglected since the end of the

On March 3, 1922, Streetcar #4, unable to make the sharp turn onto the Traffic Bridge at the bottom of the Long Hill, ran off the tracks and plunged to the river bank below. None of the twenty-eight passengers aboard were killed, and only six were injured seriously enough to be hospitalized. *Photo LH 996 by Boyles Ltd., courtesy SPL – LHR*

boom in 1913. With the exception of sporadic maintenance and the odd bit of boulevard planting, no work was done on the city's parks until 1927. That year, workers began grading and planting trees in what is now Kinsmen Park. In 1928, the Parks Board planted ten thousand trees and shrubs in Saskatoon. A new civic nursery was built at Avenue P and 33rd Street, and work began on the beautification of the downtown riverbank. By 1930 the city had 600 acres of parkland in fifteen parks, with an additional 180 acres designated later that year for future park development.

The Riversdale Swimming Pool in Victoria Park was completed in 1926. Unheated and lacking in concrete aprons (it was surrounded by a sand "beach" until the 1930s), it had its own peculiar aroma, a result of the primitive filtration system and a somewhat hit-and-miss system of chlorination. Nevertheless, the "Avenue Itch Pool," as it was sometimes known, was a huge improvement over the somewhat dangerous boomed-off section of riverbank that had earlier served the citizens of Saskatoon.

Aviation – little more than a novelty in 1914 – had come of age during the war. The earliest commercial venture in Saskatoon was McClelland Aviation, which operated out of a hangar on the western outskirts of the city at the beginning of the decade. At about the same time, the Chinese Nationalist League's Keng Wah School of Aviation was training pilots in Saskatoon for Sun Yat-sen's Republican flying corps in China. In 1928, the Saskatoon Aero Club established the city's first "air harbour," which later became the Saskatoon airport. The club (later the Saskatoon Flying Club) was the second largest in Canada by the end of 1929 and included the first woman in Saskatchewan to get a pilot's licence, Nellie Carson.

Sports, recreation, and leisure-time activities flourished in Saskatoon during the 1920s. The elegant Capitol Theatre opened at 127 2nd Avenue South in 1929. Commercial radio came to town in 1923 with the opening of CFQC, operating out of a small building on Osler Street, just south of the University. By 1925, Saskatoon had three radio stations. Semi-professional baseball and hockey games drew large crowds. In 1928 Saskatoon's darling, high jumper Ethel Catherwood, set a world's record when she won the gold medal at the Olympics in Amsterdam. The temperance issue was finally decided in 1924 when government liquor stores were allowed to open again.

A less-than-welcome addition to Saskatoon's social and political scene in the 1920s was the Ku Klux Klan. Imported into Canada from the United States (where it was failing as a political movement), the Klan had its greatest success in rural Saskatchewan, where it targeted primarily Roman Catholics, French Canadians (and the French language generally), and Eastern European immigrants. On October 18, 1927, Klan organizer J. J. Maloney came to Saskatoon to speak at the Old Knox Hall. What effect his speech had is unclear. Although the Klan claimed responsibility for the defeat of the Liberal government in the 1929 provincial election, interest in Saskatoon appears to have been limited at best, and Maloney very soon departed.

Telegraph operators at their desks in the former Canadian Northern Railway station downtown in 1923. It had been renamed the Canadian National Railways (CNR) station earlier that year, following the nationalization of the Canadian Northern and Grand Trunk railways. *Photo RB 2237 courtesy Sask Archives*

The first half of the 1920s was characterized by a slow economic recovery and varying degrees of social and political unrest. By 1925, wages and prices had stabilized, the social issues that marked the first part of the decade had been largely resolved, and for a while at least peace and prosperity descended on the city. After all those years of boom, bust, war, and turmoil, it must have been a welcome relief.

Then came the 1930s.

Looking east along 21st Street from 3rd Avenue in 1925. The building on the corner contained the City Health Department. The Saskatoon Public Library was housed in the Great War Veterans Association building next door. Beyond (left to right) are the courthouse, Masonic Temple, and the Oddfellows Hall (now Mykonos Restaurant). *Photo PH 88-366 courtesy* SPL – LHR

The Saskatoon Sanatorium, constructed in 1925 on the west side of the river south of the city, was one of a number of provincial facilities built here during this period. Others included the Normal School (now the A. E. Davies Centre) on Avenue A and the School for the Deaf (now the R.J.D. Williams Building) on Cumberland Avenue, just south of the university. Although the other two are still standing, the sanatorium was demolished in 1989. The Quaker Oats plant and King George School are in the right background. *Photo B 678 by Leonard Hillyard, courtesy* SPL – LHR

In 1928, the buildings at the corner of 3rd Avenue and 21st Street were demolished to make way for the T. Eaton Co. department store (now the Public School Board offices). The J. H. Early Motor Co. next door was one of the largest of the many automobile dealerships in the city at that time. *Photo A 1245 by Leonard Hillyard, courtesy* SPL – LHR

Looking east from the roof of the recently completed Chemistry Building (Thorvaldson Building) at some of the buildings around the "bowl" on the University campus in 1924. *Photo A 178 courtesy U of S Archives*

The majestic Spanish-Mediterranean styled lobby of the Capitol Theatre, at 182 2nd Avenue South. It led to the equally grand, similarly decorated foyer and auditorium beyond the doors at the top of the stairs. The Capitol opened in 1929 and was a popular venue for both live performances and movies for half a century. It and the Bank of Nova Scotia next door were demolished in 1979 to make way for the Scotia Centre. *Photo A 2050 by Leonard Hillyard, courtesy* SPL – LHR

The 1926-27 Saskatoon Sheiks hockey club, which played briefly in the Western Professional Hockey League, poses in front of the Crescent Rink. It had been built on the site of the former Auditorium Roller Rink on Spadina Crescent East a few years earlier. A number of these players would go on to play in the newly formed National Hockey League. *Photo LH 4137 courtesy* SPL – LHR

The Armistice Day ceremonies on November 11, 1929, were marked by the official unveiling of the cenotaph at 21st Street and 2nd Avenue. Built as a memorial to those killed in the Great War of 1914-1918, it was moved to its present location in front of city hall in 1957. *Photo A 275 by Leonard Hillyard, courtesy* SPL – LHR

The Civic Bathing Pool (now Riversdale Swimming Pool) was constructed by the city just north of the water plant, replacing the designated swimming area in the river below. It opened on July 15, 1925. *Photo PH 93-166-20 courtesy* SPL – LHR

The outdoor rink on campus, just east of the Engineering Building, is the setting of this informal scrimmage by a group of students during the winter of 1921. In 1929, it was replaced by Rutherford Rink, an indoor hockey arena. *Photo A 1034 courtesy U of S Archives*

George Bartlett, an early radio broadcast technician in Saskatoon, seated in the doorway of the CFQC transmitter building, ca 1929. It was then located on the northwest corner of the exhibition grounds. CFQC Radio had been established in 1923 by A. A. Murphy, the co-owner of the Electric Shop at 216 1st Avenue North (later the studios of CFQC Television). *Photo PH 93-83-3 by Seymour's Photo, courtesy* SPL – LHR

The crew of a snowplough pause for a photo while clearing the streetcar tracks to Sutherland, following a memorable snowstorm on March 15, 1927. *Photo LH 999 by Gibson Photos, courtesy* SPL – LHR

"The Saskatoon Lily," Ethel Catherwood, a member of the first graduating class of Bedford Road Collegiate, brought the city international renown by winning the gold medal for high jump at the 1928 Amsterdam Olympics. She is shown with Ross Brown, her publicity manager. *Photo LH 3473 by Alexandra Studios (Toronto), courtesy* SPL – LHR

Ken Peaker's Orchestra, shown here in the Palm Room in Campbell's Café (next to the King George Hotel on 2nd Avenue North), was one of a number of dance bands that played in Saskatoon nightspots from the late twenties through the thirties. Ken Peaker is second from the left. *Photo LH 3921 courtesy* SPL – LHR

In 1929, the City of Saskatoon built a Municipal Air Harbour with a small terminal building and graded runways on the site established earlier by the Saskatoon Aero Club. It was to serve the increasing commercial air transport, including airmail delivery after 1930, and is now the J. D. Diefenbaker International Airport. *Photo LH 1293 courtesy* SPL – LHR

The wreckage of a Gypsy Moth biplane belonging to the Saskatoon Aero Club lies in the river near the CPR bridge. On August 5, 1929, instructor J. E. Smith-Marriot and his passenger were killed when the plane crashed after hitting electrical wires stretched across the river from Queen Street toward Sutherland. *Photo LH 3114 courtesy* SPL – LHR

The 1929 Saskatoon Exhibition parade, moving north on 2nd Avenue, drew a large number of spectators from the city and surrounding district. The floats show the confidence local businesses had in Saskatoon's productive capacity and potential at the time. It was to be shaken a couple of months later by the onset of the Great Depression. The Metropolitan Store (left) occupies the site on which the present Scotia Bank now stands. *Photo A 935 by Leonard Hillyard, courtesy* SPL – LHR

McGAVIN'S
BREAD
DON'T SAY BREAD
SAY
McGAVIN'S
BAKERIES LTD.
McGAVIN BAKER

Chapter Five

1930-1939

When the US stock market collapsed on October 29, 1929, it took the world's economies with it, triggering the decade-long human tragedy called the Great Depression. On the prairies, the effects of the Depression were exacerbated by a drought of unprecedented magnitude.

The effects were not initially felt in Saskatoon. While unemployment at the end of 1929 was double what it had been the year before, the numbers themselves were fairly low, and in any case nothing like they had been in the years immediately after the First World War. If the value of building permits issued was any indicator of economic activity, 1930 was nearly as good year as 1929, which had been a very good year indeed. At a conference on unemployment held in Winnipeg in the summer of 1930, Mayor John Hair confidently declared that the situation in Saskatoon was under control.

He was terribly wrong. "When America sneezed," as the saying went, "the world caught a cold." In a global economy dependent on a fragile construction of inflated share prices, unsecured loans, and blind optimism, one sneeze could go a long way. In the fall of 1930, the price of wheat began to drop.

Opposite page: McGavin's Bakery (now Earl's Restaurant and Lounge), built in the Spanish style popular in the late twenties, was completed at 2nd Avenue and Queen Street in 1930. Horse-drawn delivery wagons provided homes with coal, wood, bread, and milk at the time, but declined in the years to come, ending with the last milk deliveries in 1962. *Photo B 1567 by Leonard Hillyard, courtesy* SPL – LHR

The Bessborough Hotel under construction on the river bank at the east end of 21st Street East. Started in 1929, it was to be one of several deluxe hotels the CNR was constructing across the country. Its opening was delayed until 1935 due to the onset of the Depression. *Photo C 51 by Gibson Photo, courtesy SPL – LHR*

By December it was fifty-nine cents a bushel – well below the cost of production – and it just kept dropping. In Saskatchewan, where the difference between feast and famine was inextricably linked to the price of wheat, it spelled disaster.

The Depression affected different people in different ways. Although wages dropped, prices dropped even faster. Property owners and those with jobs sometimes found themselves better off than before. For young people, farmers, small business people, and the growing legions of unemployed workers, it was the worst of times.

The city opened a relief camp for single unemployed men on the exhibition grounds during the winter of 1930-1931. There were five hundred families on relief in the spring of 1931, up from fifty the year before, and the cost to the city soared: from $4,000 in 1930 to $163,000 in 1932, when 20 per cent of the city's population was on relief. In 1935, with its own revenues seriously undercut through loss of taxes, the city paid nearly $300,000 of a total unemployment relief bill of $750,000 (which it shared with the provincial and federal governments).

The city's population dropped by 1,500 between the 1931 and 1936 censuses. It rallied again at the end of the decade, and in 1941 the figure stood at 43,027, for a net population loss of not quite 200 persons since 1931.

Neither the civic, provincial, nor federal governments seemed capable of responding effectively to the crisis. The rising costs of the disaster quickly overwhelmed existing relief measures. Governments were slow to act, and when they did their responses often seemed to be driven more by ideology and fear than by common sense and compassion. Even the most creative solutions were often so poorly administered as to make them nearly useless.

Public works projects provided the married unemployed with at least the semblance of an income (while satisfying the moral imperative that it be worked for). The 19th Street subway and the Broadway Bridge were the most ambitious of these, with most of the funding coming from the federal and provincial governments. Other projects included the digging of storm sewers and the construction of river bank improvements as well as day-labour work, generally of the unskilled variety.

After 1932, the federal government focused its relief efforts on controlling the growing army of single, homeless unemployed men. Denied assistance of any sort from local governments and feared for the threat they posed to public order, they were forced into federally run work camps such as the one near Dundurn, which was one of the largest in Canada. There they cut wood, built roads, and performed other such work for twenty cents a day. Conditions were miserable, and the camps quickly became hotbeds of unrest and political activism. Some men chose to chance starvation rather than submit to the regimentation of the "slave camps."

A store window display sponsored by the Relief Bureau. By 1932, it was apparent that the city's Relief Board couldn't meet the demand on its limited resources, so six local service clubs set up the Relief Bureau to canvass for used clothing to be distributed among the most needy families in the city. *Photo A 1419 by Leonard Hillyard, courtesy SPL – LHR*

The provincial government (acting through a local committee) tried to resettle destitute Saskatoon families onto farmsteads, where they might at least be able to raise their own food. Start-up loans were provided for seed, stock, and equipment. These farm resettlement schemes proved to be almost completely futile, costing more to administer than they saved in relief costs. Somewhat more successful was the vacant lot gardening scheme. Starting in 1934, the city rented out vacant lots for gardening purposes at a rate of fifteen cents a lot. The scheme was well received, but success depended on adequate rainfall, and in a dry year many found that the gardens involved a great deal of effort for very little return.

In 1932, the administration of direct relief in Saskatoon fell to the

Adjoining photos provide a panoramic view of houses on Avenue L North, ca. 1930, then the western fringe of the city. Plans to extend sewer and water services as well as make street improvements to areas such as this were postponed due to civic cutbacks. *Photos PH 95-78-22A & 22B by Nicholas Wen, courtesy SPL – LHR*

Civic Relief Board. Horrific stories circulated amongst the unemployed of the board's agents being paid bounties for the number of families they could have stricken from the rolls, and of men cut off relief for accepting as little as twenty-five cents in payment for doing odd jobs. The board's heavy-handed attempts to limit spending and curb perceived abuses only exacerbated the misery caused by the Depression and led to an increase in political and social ferment in the city. This included Saskatoon's first sit-in, a thirty-hour invasion of city council chambers by women protesting inadequate relief payments and the harsh and demeaning treatment they received at the hands of the relief authorities.

The women's sit-in was peaceful. Not so two weeks earlier when a club-wielding force of ninety police, RCMP, and special constables engaged a crowd of mostly single unemployed men in running battle that went from the Relief Store at 19th Street and 1st Avenue, up 19th to the subway, and finally ended at the City Market on Avenue A (now Idylwyld Drive) and 21st Street. The newspaper reported a dozen or more injured in the fracas (none seriously) and half a dozen arrests.

When the Civic Relief Board's two-year term ended in 1934, it was quietly replaced with the Relief Appeals Board, a committee of council. Worsening conditions and a growing realization that this was a crisis with no obvious end had resulted, perhaps, in a less inflexible and more realistic response from government to the needs of its citizens.

As the decade progressed, people did their best to find ways to weather the storm. Destitute men "rode the rails" looking for work, and whole families took to the road in search of greener pastures. People took in boarders to help reduce housing costs, and families moved into other people's basements or took up quarters in back yard garages. At the city's only public swimming pool, admission was five cents if you had it and free if you didn't. The meagre relief payments provided to the unemployed were also supplemented by the work of private charities such as the Salvation Army and the city's service clubs, but the pickings were nevertheless slim.

Not all was doom and desperation. The Saskatoon Technical Institute was built in 1931 on what had once been Saskatoon's Chinatown, along 19th Street downtown. Another welcome addition to the city's economic base was the Hi-Way Refinery, built in 1932 on 11th Street West. Eventually it would become one of the city's largest industrial employers. The Bessborough Hotel, Sask- atoon's castle on the river, opened after much delay in 1935, and in 1939-1940 the weir was built across the river near 33rd Street. Intended primarily to create a reservoir and to help control water levels, it also created a landing basin for pontoon- equipped aircraft in the unlikely event that one should ever come looking for a place to touch down in Saskatoon.

One of the brighter moments of the 1930s was the opening of the Saskatoon Arena on 19th Street near 1st Avenue. Financed through public subscription and built with the help of donated materials and labour (including $13,000 worth of relief labour provided by the city and the province), it was a true example of what they used to call "Saskatoon spirit": the ability of people to work together to overcome adversity through sheer determination.

In large ways and small the people of Saskatoon worked together to see it through. By 1938, prices were starting to rise and the wheels of industry were slowly beginning to turn once more. It seemed finally that there might be some respite on the horizon. In June of 1939, the king and queen visited a city turned out in its best clothes to cheer on the royal couple. A new decade was in the offing, and perhaps with it a new beginning.

Then, on September 1, 1939, the Nazi blitzkrieg ravened across the borders of Poland. Ten days later, for the second time in a generation, Canada – and Saskatoon – was again marching to war in Europe.

A shack made of packing crates on the east bank of the river just north of the CPR Bridge in 1931. This was one of a number of such temporary dwellings along the river that were used by destitute individuals at the time. *Photo LH 2048 by the Saskatoon* StarPhoenix, *courtesy* SPL – LHR

The Technical Collegiate – Saskatoon's first vocational school – under construction on the site of the former Chinatown at 19th Street and 3rd Avenue about 1930. On November 7, 1932, a joint force of the city police and RCMP forcibly removed a group of unemployed men who had gathered on the school grounds. *Photo LH 4424 by John W. Gibson, courtesy SPL – LHR*

The RCMP mounted squad, lined up on Avenue B North, just prior to a confrontation on November 8, 1932, at Market Square (now the site of No. 1 Fire Station) with unemployed men who were protesting their accommodations in the government relief camp at the exhibition grounds. Four protesters were arrested. No serious injuries were reported. *Photo NA-2796-31 courtesy of Glenbow Archives*

An early physical education class in the gymnasium of the Technical Collegiate, then the most spacious gym in the city. *Photo A 1026 by Leonard Hillyard, courtesy* SPL – LHR

Looking east at the new subway under the CNR tracks at 19th Street. The subway was constructed in 1931, to replace one close to Spadina Crescent. It was financed by senior governments as a make-work project. The inclines were paved with cobblestones (right foreground) to provide traction for horses to pull vehicles up the grade. *Photo PH 91-179-31 by Nelson Warner, courtesy* SPL – LHR

Constructing the roadbed of the Broadway Bridge. Conceived as a make-work project for men on relief, it was designed by engineers from the University of Saskatchewan and built by local contractors using local unemployed men. It opened in 1932. Streetcar lines were rerouted from the Traffic Bridge to the Broadway Bridge the following year. The Crescent Rink had to be demolished for the roadway connecting the bridge with 19th Street. *Photo A 184 by Leonard A. Hillyard, courtesy* SPL – LHR

The Quakers hockey club, the provincial senior champion, on a float in the 1933 Travellers Day parade. The following year, the Quakers represented Canada in the World Amateur Championship in Milan, Italy, defeating the USA 2-1 in the final. Local games were played in Exhibition Stadium (since demolished) on the exhibition grounds between 1931 and 1937. *Photo LH 3558 by Leonard Hillyard, courtesy* SPL – LHR

A group of onlookers gather near a plane that made an emergency landing on the frozen river near the Water Treatment Plant on January 18, 1932. Smoke from the A. L. Cole Power Plant rises above the city beyond the CNR bridge in the middle. This plant was the former Saskatoon Power Station, which had been incorporated into the Saskatchewan Power Commission in 1928. *Photo PH 2002-15-1 courtesy* SPL – LHR

In September 1937, the Saskatoon Arena, hailed as the only artificial ice surface between Winnipeg and Calgary, opened on 19th Street next to the Technical School. Built by a volunteer committee that sold shares to local residents and handled the contracts for the construction, it was a manifestation of "Saskatoon Spirit" at work. The city took over the arena in 1958. It closed in 1988 and was torn down the following year. Clinkskill Manor seniors' residence now occupies the site. *Photo LH 8549 courtesy* SPL – LHR

Matches underway at the Riversdale Lawn Bowling Green in Victoria Park (north of the water plant on Avenue H), ca. 1935. The Saskatoon Brewing Company (later Labatt's) is visible (left background) across the river. *Photo LH 5264 by Helen Schrader, courtesy* SPL – LHR

The Huskies basketball team plays in the cramped quarters of the Qu'Appelle Hall gym, ca. 1930. Building on the university campus was severely curtailed throughout the decade due to provincial cutbacks. *Photo A 8028 courtesy U of S Archives*

The Gray Goose Stage, ca. 1935, parked in front of the Union Bus Depot at 347 2nd Avenue South. The Black And White Cab Co. began serving the larger communities of central Saskatchewan in 1931. In 1934, it amalgamated with Arrow Coach Lines, making it part of a much larger passenger transport network. *Photo A 1660 by Leonard Hillyard, courtesy* SPL – LHR

The Saskatoon Symphony Orchestra on stage in Convocation Hall in the College Building on the university campus in 1933. This is one example of the cooperation and good relations between "town and gown" through the years. *Photo LH 822 courtesy* SPL – LHR

Movies, such as these showing, ca. 1937, at the Roxy Theatre on 20th Street West, were a welcome diversion from the economic woes of the time. The Roxy (completed in 1929), like the Capitol, was built in the Spanish style popular at the time. The interior had a Spanish villa décor with a domed skylike ceiling through which star lights blinked on and off. It was operated as the Towne Cinema from 1974 to 1995. It was restored to some of its original grandeur and reopened as a "second run" theatre in 2005. *Photo PH 91-179-6 by Nelson Warner, courtesy* SPL – LHR

The weir near 33rd Street in 1939. It was constructed to stabilize water levels in the river, with federal funding provided under the Prairie Farm Rehabilitation Authority (PFRA). The ski jump on the east bank (right background) had been moved from its original location on the University campus in 1930. *Photo PH 2002-141-24-2 courtesy* SPL – LHR

Looking north on Broadway from 8th Street as crowds disperse following the passing of the Saskatoon Exhibition parade in 1935. The Red Robin Café (left middle ground) was a popular hangout for university students and local residents. *Photo LH 4282 by John W. Gibson, courtesy* SPL – LHR

King George VI and Queen Elizabeth stand on the platform at the back of their special train as it leaves Saskatoon following their royal visit on June 3, 1939. The Saskatoon Brewing Company building (later Labatt's) in the background was demolished in 1993. It is now the site of the River Landing condominiums. *Photo A 1077 by Leonard Hillyard, courtesy* SPL – LHR

Chapter 6

1940-1949

On September 10, 1939, Canada declared war on Nazi Germany. With only 4,500 regular armed forces personnel, some 50,000 or so partly trained reservists, and an almost-complete absence of modern equipment, the Canadian military was woefully unprepared. Nevertheless, just as they had in 1914, the men – and women – of Saskatoon flocked to join up. The Saskatoon Light Infantry (successor to the earlier 105th Regiment Fusiliers) was mobilized immediately and two months later set sail for England. Men who had survived the "war to end all wars" in 1918 now watched as their own sons donned uniforms and marched off to a new war in Europe. By war's end, men and women from Saskatoon could be found in every service of the country's armed forces.

Membership in either the sea, army, or air cadet corps was made compulsory for physically fit male students attending Saskatoon's high schools. Sea cadets attended training camps on Shepley Island on the river south of Saskatoon. Naval and air training units were also established at the University of Saskatchewan to supplement the existing Canadian Officer Training Corps program. Military sci-

Opposite page: The 1st Battalion of the Saskatoon Light Infantry (SLI) left Saskatoon in December 1939 to become part of the 1st Division of the Canadian Expeditionary Force to England. In this photograph, family and friends see off another company of the SLI at the CPR station in the fall of 1942. It was bound for further training in eastern Canada before being shipped overseas as a part of a 1st Division support battalion. *Photo COTC fonds, file no. 16, by Percy Shore, courtesy U of S Archives*

The pavement at 21st Street and 1st Avenue formed the parade ground for Saskatoon's naval detachment, ca. 1943. Alongside them is Tom Guest's service station. Great West Saddlery (in the former Hutchings building) and Ashdown Hardware loom in the background. When a devastating fire destroyed an earlier version of the J. H. Ashdown warehouse on March 18, 1918, the adjoining Great West Saddlery was partially damaged too. Another spectacular fire destroyed the second Ashdown building (housing Uncle Ed's Furniture) on October 8, 1996. *Photo A 665 by Leonard Hillyard, courtesy* SPL – LHR

ence and other technical courses were offered as well as courses for women, including wartime fundraising, sewing and knitting for the Red Cross, first aid, motor maintenance, and office work. Facilities for radio and electronics training were also provided at the Technical Collegiate.

In the fall of 1940, the federal government took over Saskatoon's airport to build a training base for the newly formed British Commonwealth Air Training Plan. Under the plan, air force recruits from across the British Commonwealth (primarily Canada, Great Britain, Australia, and New Zealand) would be trained in Canada at schools operated by the Royal Canadian Air Force. A second BCATP facility – the No. 7 Initial Training School – opened in 1941 next to the Normal School on Avenue A, on the site of the present-day Kelsey Campus of SIAST.

The influx of recruits from all the services strained Saskatoon at the seams. New hangars and barracks were built at the airport and next to the Normal School to accommodate the BCATP trainees. Bedford Road Collegiate was used as a training centre, as were the exhibition grounds, including the stadium and grandstand. A variety of local buildings were requisitioned for use as storage depots. In 1943 the Royal Canadian Naval Reserve, which had been operating out of a car dealership on 1st Avenue North and 25th Street, moved to a new building (now the HMCS Unicorn) on land donated by the city at 4th Avenue and 24th Street, across from city hall. Many men were billeted with Saskatoon families. In all, some 7,000 military personnel of all services were stationed in Saskatoon at one time or another during the war.

Fundraising was an important part of the war effort, and in this area too Saskatoon shone. The people of Saskatoon donated a tank to the Free French, and city council made a gift to the crew of the corvette HMCS Saskatoon of 17,400 cigarettes, four radios, a washing machine, and a subscription to *Life* magazine in addition to sewing kits, ashtrays, playing cards, and other such items. The RCAF's 406 (Lynx) Squadron – adopted by the City of Saskatoon and later to be called the City of Saskatoon Squadron – did somewhat better, receiving 100,000 cigarettes and 425 Christmas parcels as well as three subscriptions to the *Star-Phoenix* newspaper (but no washing machine, and to be fair, the 406 Squadron fundraiser was helped out by money raised by the Saskatoon Air Force Auxiliary).

Other fundraising efforts included the Victory Loan campaign, "tag days" put on by different organizations raising money for various causes, and the "Stamp Out the U-Boats" campaign to buy depth charges for the Canadian Navy.

Rationing was a fact of life in Saskatoon during the war. The federal Wartime Prices and Trade Board instituted food rationing in January 1942. Tea, coffee, sugar, and butter were rationed first, followed in 1943 by meat and preserves. Gasoline was rationed beginning in the spring of 1942. The demands of war meant that many articles, including silk stockings and canned foods, were almost impossible to obtain. Canadians were urged to "Use it up, wear it out, make it do, and do without." Recycling was also big. The Cosmopolitan Club organized scrap drives, circulating flyers asking people to donate rubber goods, fat drippings, bones, metals, bottles, glass, various textiles, used clothing, carpets, mattresses, draperies, and jute bags. All of these had value of one sort or another to the war effort.

The people of Saskatoon were affected by the war in other ways. Here, as in the rest of Canada, women stepped up to fill the jobs left vacant by men suddenly in uniform. Women also served in the armed forces – albeit in strictly auxiliary roles – and in 1942 a squadron of the RCAF Women's Division was stationed in Saskatoon. Women weren't the only ones called on to serve in unexpected ways. Acute labour shortages in rural Saskatchewan meant that during harvest, businessmen, office workers, and students left

Passersby in downtown Saskatoon must have been startled by this "invasion" of military trucks and tanks in October 1942, when army personnel in training staged a "blitz" on city streets. In the background is the Bowerman Block (occupied by Caswell's men's clothing store) on 21st Street East near 2nd Avenue. *Photo COTC fonds, file no. 16, by Percy Shore, courtesy U of S Archives*

An upper floor of the Birks building at 3rd Avenue and 21st Street downtown was taken over temporarily by the RCAF as a recruiting station during the war. Skilled tradesmen with only a grade eight education could get into the force, but would-be pilots and observers needed grade eleven to qualify. *Photo B 2890 by Leonard Hillyard, courtesy SPL – LHR*

their classrooms and offices to help bring in the crops. Citizens also practised emergency civil defence procedures, air raid drills, and blackouts.

Germany formally surrendered on May 8, 1945, and Japan on August 15. The war was over. Over a million Canadians had served full-time in the armed forces, mostly in Europe. Many had been overseas for more than five years, and now it was time to bring them home. The Saskatoon Light Infantry returned in October, and by early 1946 most Canadian soldiers were home.

Great efforts were made to integrate returning soldiers back into civilian life. Returning veterans were given a year's university credits for active service and offered rapid matriculation classes and a host of practical courses to ease their transition back into society. The university paid their fees and provided a monthly living allowance. With university residences overflowing, the barracks of the former BCATP schools at the airport and by the Normal School on Avenue A accommodated the expanded student population. Surplus air force hangars and barracks were moved to the campus to house classes, laboratories, and offices, and one of them – known as the Hangar Building – served the Drama Department and Greystone Theatre until 1994.

Given their long sojourn overseas, it should come as no surprise that many returning soldiers brought wives and children back with them. Some 48,000 "war brides," most of them British, came to Canada after the war, bringing with them more than 22,000 children. By the summer of 1946 about 134 war brides had arrived in Saskatoon, many with babies.

By war's end, the city's population had swelled to more than 50,000, resulting in a significant housing crisis. Very little new building had occurred in the city since the early 1930s, and now the available housing stock was almost non-existent. Several hundred new homes were built with federal assistance under the Wartime Housing Act on land supplied by the city in various areas. Most of these compact but serviceable "wartime" houses survive to this day. On the far western fringe of the city, the Veterans Land Administration community of Montgomery began to be built on land that had originally been subdivided during the pre-First World War real estate boom. Veterans were given low interest loans and grants with which to set up small agricultural holdings, including garden plots and livestock. Montgomery's half-acre lots were admirably suited to this purpose, and while the VLA land scheme was not completely successful, the community that grew up at the end of 11th Street West had a small-town character all its own.

Despite rationing and shortages, local industries had been running at capacity to meet wartime demands. New businesses like Intercontinental Packers, founded by Czechoslovakian refugee Fred Mendel, were established, and existing ones like Canada Egg Producers expanded. The discovery and exploitation of new uranium, potash, and oil resources as well as the growth of lumbering and fishing and other new industries in the province all added to a growing prosperity in Saskatoon. While coal – which most people used to heat their houses – was scarce, there was talk of an oil and gas pipeline to supply the city's energy demands.

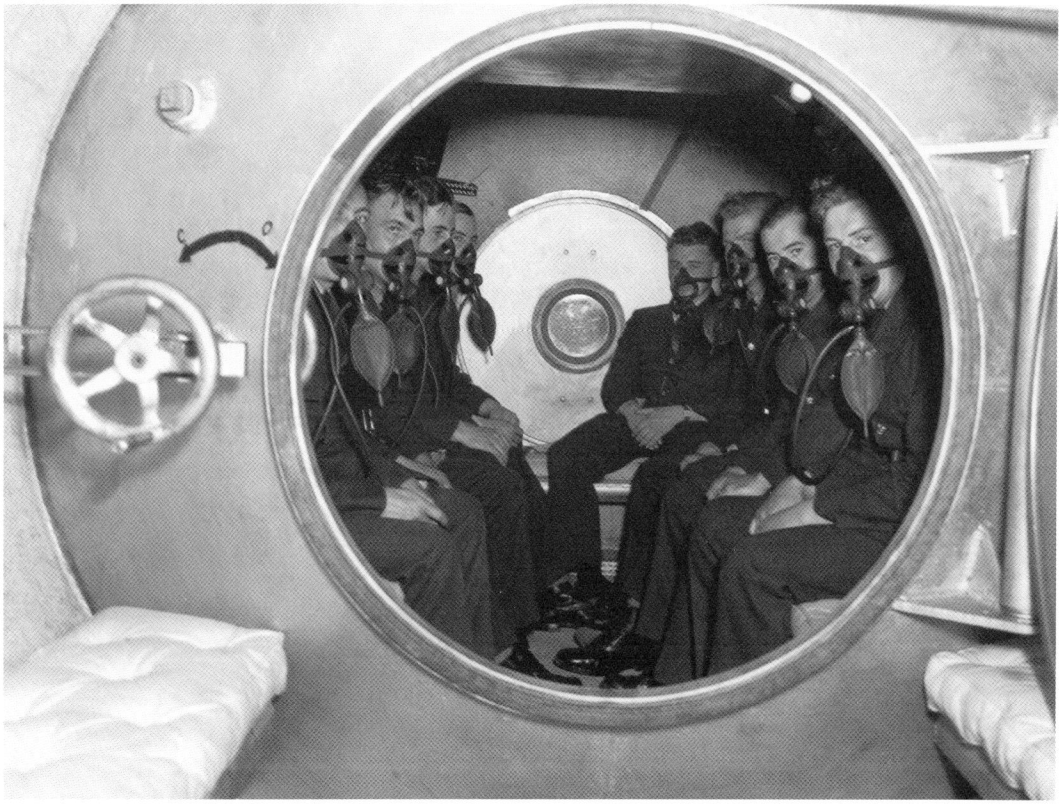

Aircrew trainees wear oxygen masks in a decompression chamber in the medical building of the Initial Training School in June 1941. The ITS was part of the British Commonwealth Air Training Plan, which trained students from around the world at centres across Canada. This training module simulated the thin air at altitudes up to 25,000 feet. *Photo B 2863 by Leonard Hillyard, courtesy SPL – LHR*

Finally, after all the wartime deprivations, Saskatoon was bathed in optimism. Prices were high, profit margins were secure, harvests were good, and jobs were available. The war was over and the harrowing times of the Dirty Thirties were long past. The future looked rosy.

The number of uniformed military personnel in Saskatoon during the war years is apparent in this photo of the opening of a hockey game in the Arena Rink in the early 1940s. The sign under the clock states, "Now is the time to buy Victory Bonds." *Photo A 665 by Leonard Hillyard, courtesy* SPL – LHR

This Four Freedoms Tableau in Kiwanis Park was part of a huge public relations campaign to raise funds for the war effort. The *StarPhoenix* devoted most of its third page to the pageant, which despite a chilling wind had taken place May 9, 1943. *Photo A 1075 by Leonard Hillyard, courtesy* SPL – LHR

Parade floats like this, urging the purchase of war savings stamps, helped heighten public approval for the war effort, encouraging enlistments, fundraising, and other efforts on the home front. German U-boats (submarines) were a continuing threat to Allied shipping and navies. This July 1942 shot shows 2nd Avenue South between 21st and 22nd Street East. At the far left is Golf's Chocolate Shop, a popular gathering place, and Success Business College. Note the wartime use of horses instead of motor vehicles. *Photo B 3011 by Leonard Hillyard, courtesy* SPL – LHR

The tank presented to the forces of Free France on behalf of the inhabitants of Saskatoon. It was financed with funds raised from the "Buy a Tank" campaign launched by a local volunteer committee in June 1940. *Photo HST-031 courtesy City of Saskatoon Archives*

Cairns Field on Avenue A (now Idylwyld Drive) near Walmer Road and the CPR tracks, ca. 1943, remained a conveniently located baseball facility, floodlit for evening games. In 1924, the Elks Lodge leased Cairns Field and ran it until 1932. The Saskatoon Ball League took over the lease from 1933 until 1935, followed by W. H. Burneice and subsequently his widow, until 1949. Then the Saskatoon Playgrounds Association purchased and ran the facility for the city. The field was dismantled in 1963, to make way for the widening of Avenue A. *Photo LH 6326 courtesy SPL – LHR*

Teenaged Gordie Howe stands in the back row, third from right, with his teammates on the King George Athletic Club bantam hockey team in March 1942. Mr. and Mrs. Bert Hodges were coach and team manager of the bantam division, which they helped to organize in 1939-40. Other boys identified here include: Arto Buick, Jack Cambridge, Roy Duckworth, Lloyd Edney, Gordon Eshpeter, Ron and Tom Hodges, John Kalapaca, Bud Kobusson, Ron O'Hara, Robert Spurgeon, Everett Wilson, Ray Woolford, and Bill Yanowzeski (Yano). *Photo LH 9373 by Leonard Hillyard, courtesy SPL – LHR*

Lt. Col. Drayton Walker leads the 1st Battalion of the Saskatoon Light Infantry up 21st Street on its return to Saskatoon on October 3, 1945. The new CNR station (completed in 1939) is in the background. Following a final inspection on the Bessborough grounds, the battalion was officially dismissed. *Photo B 1732 by Leonard Hillyard, courtesy SPL – LHR*

The YWCA Traveller's Aid Society greeted returning servicemen, war brides, and children at this reception station set up in the CNR station on 1st Avenue at 21st Street. The man on the right is probably a railway porter, who helped passengers with their luggage. *Photo B 1530 by Leonard Hillyard, courtesy SPL – LHR*

Three well-known Saskatoon artists, Wynona Mulcaster, Ernest Lindner, and Robert Hurley in the Saskatoon Art Centre (in the Standard Trust Building) shortly after its opening in May 1944. This first art centre had been made possible by a grant from city council. It included a camera club darkroom and gallery as well as sketching rooms where children's art classes were conducted on Saturday mornings. *Photo PH 88-915 courtesy SPL – LHR*

Saskatoon artist Ernest Lindner demonstrates how to sketch a portrait at the Saskatoon Art Centre, ca. 1945. Bud Temple is the model, dressed in a military uniform. Dr. Leslie Saunders is in the right foreground. *Photo PH 88-917 courtesy SPL – LHR*

The Tivoli Theatre at 233 2nd Avenue South, ca. 1946. Originally the Victoria Theatre (1913), it was rebuilt in 1930 in the Spanish-Mediterranean style exemplified by the Capitol Theatre. It had been fitted for "talkies," and fire safety improvements were made. It was renovated, including the addition of a more modern-style façade, in the 1960s and operated as the Odeon Theatre. It and part of the former Bank of Canada building (left) is now the Odeon events centre. *Photo B 163 by Leonard Hillyard, courtesy* SPL – LHR

Can-can dancers on stage at "23 Skidoo," a Jewish Variety Night held at the Empire Theatre for a B'nai B'rith convention in 1948. The Empire Theatre closed a few years later and was torn down in 1958. *Photo PH 96-38-79 by Eugene Boyko, courtesy* SPL – LHR

Members of the Saskatoon Sea Cadet Corps wash clothes at the Navy League of Canada (Saskatchewan Division) camp on Shepley Island (now Wilson Island) south of the city in August 1946. This camp for boys twelve years and older operated each summer between 1943 and 1948. *Photo B 5799 by Leonard Hillyard, courtesy* SPL – LHR

A procession of First Communicants accompanied by their teachers (Sisters of Sion) proceeds north on Avenue O from St. Mary's School to St. Mary's Church, ca. 1948. The distinctive domes of St. George's Ukrainian Catholic Cathedral, at Avenue M and 20th Street West, are in the background. *Photo B 577 by Leonard Hillyard, courtesy SPL – LHR*

Renowned university track coach E. W. (Joe) Griffiths fires the starting pistol to launch the Gil Watson Annual Torch Race at "Grifffiths' Rally," which was part of annual frosh week celebrations, ca. 1946, at the University of Saskatchewan. The university's Griffiths Stadium (constructed in 1936) was named after him. *Photo A 1087 courtesy U of S Archives*

One of the over six hundred wartime houses constructed in Saskatoon between 1944 and 1948 under the federal Wartime Housing Act. These houses were often constructed on existing empty lots along streetcar routes, such as Avenue A, Lorne Avenue, and 8th Street in the city as well as in the new Montgomery subdivision on the western outskirts. *Photo S-SP-B 2654-9 courtesy Sask Archives,* StarPhoenix *Collection*

The Little Chief service station at Avenue D and 20th Street West, ca. 1948. It was built in 1929 in the Spanish colonial style popular at the time and occupied until the 1980s. After remaining vacant for a number of years, this property was forfeited to the city. In 2004, it was designated a municipal heritage property and converted to its present use as a community police substation. *Photo A 1197 by Leonard Hillyard, courtesy SPL – LHR*

This 1949 vista confronted skiers at the top of the ski slide that once pierced the horizon on the east bank of the river, just south of the weir. Its height and steepness produced enough speed to send the skier sailing through the air and out onto the river. The skiers' clubhouse is at upper right. A commemorative plaque now marks the site of Ski Jump Coulee. *Photo A 1056 courtesy U of S Archives*

The Bessborough Hotel's ballroom has been the site of many dances over the years, both formal and informal. This one shows at least one couple doing the jitterbug, which was popular in the 1940s. *Photo B 3231 by Leonard Hillyard, courtesy* SPL – LHR

SINGLE FILE
TO THE LEFT
PLEASE
SASK.A
LOSIS LEAGUE
S CLINIC
TU
BY
SEALS
CH

Chapter Seven

1950-1959

By the 1950s, Saskatoon's wartime shortages were a thing of the past. Canada's active role in the postwar reconstruction of Europe, favourable weather and good crops in Saskatchewan, and the exploitation of new mineral resources in the Saskatoon area all helped drive the city to new economic heights. Large-scale mining of potash began in the Saskatoon area, leading the city to crown itself the Potash Capital of the World. The postwar surge in private and public building continued unabated. Money was flowing in, Saskatoon was booming, and life was good.

The population of Saskatoon almost doubled during the 1950s, to 90,000 people, making it one of the fastest growing cities in Canada. This increase – a result of both the postwar baby boom and the beginnings of the rural-urban migration that continues to this day – was to have significant and long-lasting effects on the physical and social face of the city. While university and high school enrolments doubled from 1950 to 1959, elementary school enrolments tripled, the first sign of the great population bulge that was to work its way through society in the following decades.

Opposite page: Primary students at Albert School line up for chest x-rays as part of Saskatoon's annual tuberculosis survey in September 1950. *Photo S-SP-B295-1 courtesy Sask Archives,* StarPhoenix *collection.*

Pat Fletcher (left), the club pro, and Dr. Bill Kinnear, a local pediatrician and club member, at the first tee of the Saskatoon Golf and Country Club (SGCC) course in July 1950. The SGCC hosted the Canadian Amateur Championship that year. Fletcher was the last Canadian to win the Canadian Open, Canada's premier professional tournament, held in Vancouver in 1954. *Photo B 2740 by Leonard Hillyard, courtesy SPL – LHR*

Saskatoon's physical area more than doubled during the 1950s. Annexation of surrounding farm land and of the university lands, as well as amalgamation with the town of Sutherland and the Veterans Land Administration community of Montgomery (now the Montgomery Place subdivision) added nearly 10,000 acres to the corporate area. More importantly, vast areas within city limits that had been subdivided before the First World War and never built upon were finally developed, particularly along the southeastern fringe. By 1953, the city was closing in on the "Three Sisters," a trio of identical houses on York Avenue south of Taylor Street that had sat alone far beyond the limit of the city's built-up area since the end of the 1909–1912 real estate boom. Residential planning underwent major changes during this time as well. The Grosvenor Park subdivision north of 8th Street and east of Cumberland Avenue was the first in the city to be built around a system of curving crescents rather than the traditional grid pattern, followed by other new subdivisions in the southeast including Avalon, Adelaide, and Greystone Heights.

The University of Saskatchewan was growing too, with the addition of a University Hospital in 1955 as well as Ellis Hall, the Memorial Union Building, and the St. Thomas More building, among others. The new construction on campus blended harmoniously with the existing architectural theme. Downtown, however, structures such as the new Hudson's Bay department store building and the new city hall were being built in the ultramodern International Style then in vogue. With their clean, boxlike lines, they looked startlingly plain next to the exuberant architectural detailing of their boom-era neighbours.

Other new buildings included the Queen Elizabeth power plant south of Saskatoon, Aden Bowman Collegiate, the Churchill Shopping Centre (Saskatoon's first shopping plaza), and a much-needed new terminal building at the airport. By the end of the decade, the city had five collegiates and the housing boom was still going strong, with land sales at a record $1 million. New buildings were on the drawing board: a new post office, a new Medical Arts Building, and an addition to St. Andrew's College. The university announced plans to spend $8 million on new student residences to accommodate the expected surge of new enrolments.

The number of motor vehicles in Saskatoon tripled during the 1950s, seriously overloading the capacity of the city's streets. Downtown parking was a particular problem, but just getting around was starting to become difficult. Casualties of the increased popularity of the motor vehicle included the traditional horse-drawn milk wagons (although not finally until 1962) and the old horse-drawn sidewalk snowploughs. The City of Saskatoon retired its last team of horses in 1957, the first full year of operation for the Engineering Department's new Traffic Division. The railways were feeling the heat too: by the end of the decade the CNR had reduced its passenger services to only a handful of trains and the CPR had stopped running passenger trains through Saskatoon entirely. The soaring popularity of the family car was changing the look and feel of cities around the world, Saskatoon included.

Consumer goods were once again readily available following the lifting of wartime restrictions. Here, customers crowd around the counters in Birks Jewellers on 21st Street and 3rd Avenue during a January sale in 1951. *Photo B 9733 by Leonard Hillyard, courtesy SPL – LHR*

The popularity of the automobile for leisure-time activity also brought with it increased financial opportunities, particularly in tourism. The city began planning ways to capture some of the tourist dollars moving over the nation's highways, including the building of Holiday Park (now Gordie Howe Park), a large recreational complex in the city's south west. The park was planned both as a

In August 1953, three local Olympians take part in a parade celebrating Saskatoon's founding seventy years earlier. Bob Adams (left) represented Canada in the decathlon and George Genereux (centre) won the gold medal for trap shooting at the 1952 summer games in Helsinki. Craig Mackay (right) represented Canada in speed skating in the preceding winter games. The tall building on the right is the boom-era Drinkle No. 3 Building, now Regent Plaza, at 115 3rd Avenue North. *Photo S-SP-B 1500-1 courtesy Sask Archives,* StarPhoenix *Collection*

draw for local people and as a potential tourist destination, and was to include a campground to serve the motoring public.

The Western Development Museum, which had been originally established in an old hangar near the airport, was moved in the mid-1950s to new quarters on 11th Street West. Much of the early planning for the Holiday Park area, in fact, was centred around the museum and its associated summer show, the Pion-Era Exhibition. The city's leisure facilities were greatly expanded and two new outdoor pools were built: Lathey Pool in the south and Mayfair Pool in the north.

The continuing commercial development of the 8th Street strip east from Clarence Avenue was also made possible by the increased mobility afforded by the automobile. "JDs" – a licensed restaurant far out on 8th Street where the Circle Centre Mall was later built – was extremely popular. Drive-in restaurants sprang up all along the 8th Street strip, catering to newly mobile teenagers as well as families, as did driving ranges and a miniature golf course, a roller rink, gas stations, motels, and service stations. Drive-in theatres were also immensely popular.

Saskatoon's social life and entertainment scene was booming too during the 1950s. For the high-society set, the Saskatoon Art Centre's annual Beaux Arts Ball was a not-to-be-missed event in the city's social calendar, as was the splashy affair hosted by the Women's Symphony Committee. Local fashion shows featuring models drawn from the ranks of Saskatoon's high society were also popular, as were such events as the Press Club annual ball. Naturally, all the comings and goings of the upper crust were solemnly reported in the society pages of the local newspaper. The not-so-high society set frequented dance and music venues like The Art and the Club 400. Teenage "bobby-soxers" flocked to dances in the YWCA and YMCA, HMCS Unicorn, the campus gym, and local collegiates to jive to the new music so despised by their parents. Free "bebop" concerts were held on Sunday evenings in the Kiwanis Park bandstand. Travelling troupes performed in local cinemas, as did student groups from the University of Saskatchewan and local theatre groups. Keen fans could see big American stars in the flesh, usually at the Saskatoon Arena, although the Capitol Theatre or Third Avenue United Church were more likely venues for visiting operatic singers.

In the home entertainment world, radio was still king in 1950. Most programs were imported from the United States, but local shows such as the Association of Canadian Travellers' Amateur Hour also thrived. Television arrived in 1954. CFQC – then a CBC affiliate – was for many years the only game in town. Local programming included *Sallytime,* featuring Sally Merchant, children's entertainer Helen Lumby (née Hase) and her acclaimed *Miss Helen's Kindergarten* series, and the highly derivative *Teens on TV,* in which local teenagers flaunted their jiving skills for the entertainment of the viewing audience. By the end of the decade, most homes had a television set.

Saskatoon in the 1950s was a city in transition, setting the stage for the social and cultural upheavals that were to mark the turbulent 1960s. Despite all the hijinks, the advent of the Cold War had spawned an underlying anxiety. Schools held air-raid drills, and residents became familiar with the chill sound of air raid sirens splitting the night air. Some people built fallout shelters in their basements and stocked up on canned goods and fresh water in preparation for a seemingly imminent nuclear war. Men from Saskatoon served with the United Nations in the Korean War, defending the world against the perceived threat of communist expansion. In the United States, the Red Scare was in full swing, and US Senator Joe McCarthy and the Un-American Activities Committee hearings that so galvanized the American public were front-page news here as well. But still, Saskatoon during the 1950s was a great place to be: the music was loud, the cars were fast, money was easy, and change was in the air.

The last streetcars were taken out of service in 1951. It was less expensive to extend public transit service into the new residential areas of the city with the trolley buses that replaced them. *Photo S-SP-B 47-1 courtesy Sask Archives,* StarPhoenix *Collection*

Looking north over the downtown area of Saskatoon, ca. 1954. In the left foreground are the Arena Rink and the Saskatoon Technical Collegiate which replaced earlier structures including Chinatown. The armouries and the officers' mess (the former Clinkskill House) were demolished a few years later and replaced by the present Sgt Hugh Cairns VC Armoury on Avenue A (now Idylwyld Drive) North. *Photo B 370 by Leonard A. Hillyard, courtesy* SPL – LHR

Premier T. C. Douglas welcomes "a new era for industrial expansion for Saskatoon" (and a convenience for homeowners) with the introduction of natural gas for home and commercial use on October 1, 1953. Soon after his speech, a flame was lit indicating that natural gas now filled the lines that had been installed beneath the city's streets. *Photo LH 4766 courtesy* SPL – LHR

The aerial ladder truck of the Saskatoon Fire Department leaving the No. 1 Fire Hall at 23rd Street East in February 1953. The city was quickly outgrowing the capacity of the old fire hall and that of the Public Library (which had been completed in 1929) directly to the west. *Photo B 15002 by Leonard Hillyard, courtesy* SPL – LHR

Young people jive on the set of *Teens on* TV, ca. 1959, at the studios of CFQC-TV at 216 1st Avenue North. CFQC began televising in December 1954 as a CBC affiliate. *Photo QC 1081-8 by* CFQC *staff, courtesy* SPL – LHR

A spring "dib derby," ca. 1954, sponsored by the Saskatoon Playgrounds Association on the grounds of St. Paul's High School for boys at 22nd and 4th Avenue (now the site of Federated Co-operatives Ltd.). *Photo B 829 by Leonard Hillyard, courtesy* SPL – LHR

By the fall of 1953, new residential development had reached the Three Sisters at Taylor Street and York Avenue, constructed there during the boom preceding the First World War. The concrete structures in the foreground were basements intended for other houses not yet built when the recession hit in 1913. No. 3 Fire Hall now occupies the site of the northernmost (left) of these three early houses. *Photo S-SP 2181-8 courtesy Sask Archives,* StarPhoenix *Collection*

A 1954 "freshie" class at the Saskatoon Technical Collegiate. Such hazing was a ritual experienced by freshmen at the hands of the seniors in Saskatoon high schools until the 1970s, when at the insistence of both the public and Catholic boards, it was replaced by "Welcome Week" activities. *Photo A-AP-B 2677-1 courtesy Sask Archives,* StarPhoenix *Collection*

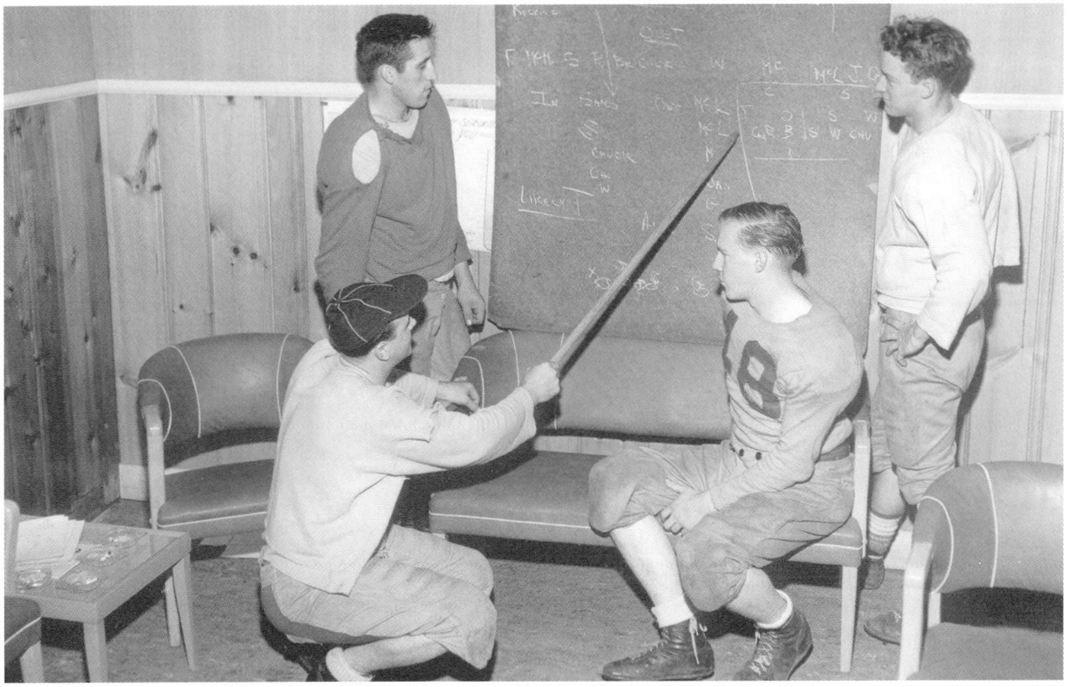

In September 1953, assistant coach Johnny Babineau explains diagrammed plays to members of the Hilltops football team in the office of their clubhouse on Kilburn Avenue (now Ron Atchison field). The players (right to left) are Chuck Boliantz, Art Risdahl, and Larry Bertell. That November the Hilltops won the Dominion Junior Football Championship, defeating the Windsor AKO 34-6 at Griffiths Stadium. *Photo S-SP 2199-1 courtesy Sask Archives,* StarPhoenix *Collection*

Max (left) and Doug Bentley played for the senior Quakers in the Western Hockey League for several years after retiring from the NHL. Here, at a game in the Saskatoon Arena during the 1954-55 season, they meet their former Chicago Blackhawks line-mate Bill Mosienko, who was playing for the Winnipeg Warriors. *Photo QC 329 by CFQC staff, courtesy SPL – LHR*

The "Coronation Calvalcade," commemorating the coronation of Queen Elizabeth II that year, proceeds around the ice surface of the elaborately decorated Arena Rink during the Saskatoon Figure Skating Club's 1954 Ice Carnival. *Photo B 12884 by Leonard Hillyard, courtesy SPL – LHR*

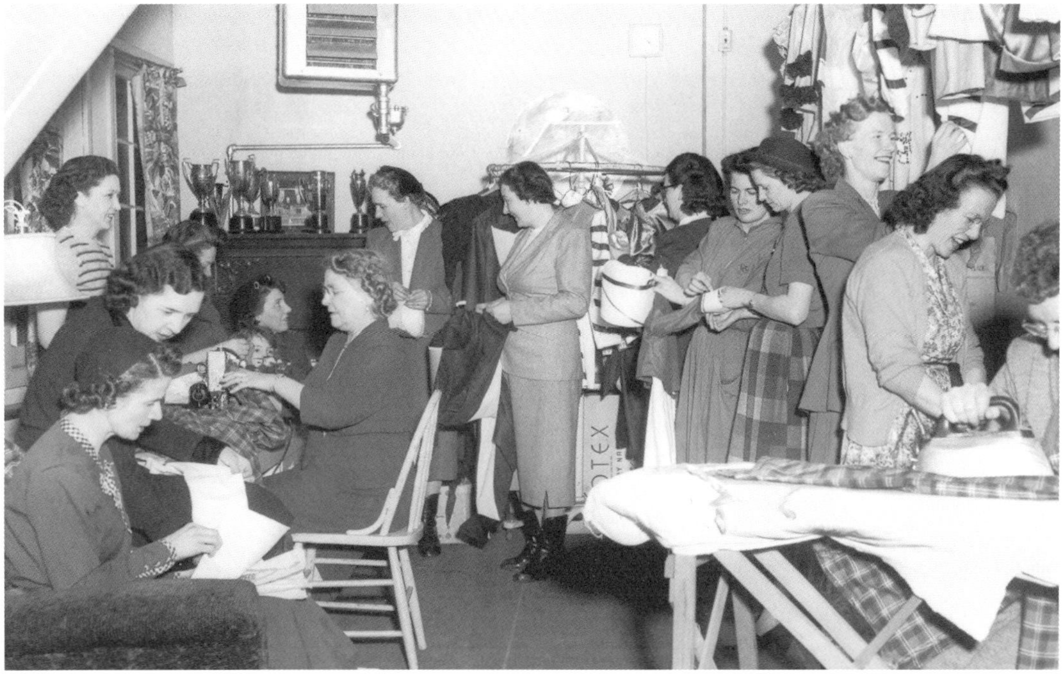

Each year, mothers such as these worked feverishly behind the scenes to make the costumes worn by the young skaters in the Saskatoon Figure Skating Club's annual Ice Carnival in 1952. *Photo B 12649 by Leonard Hillyard, courtesy* SPL – LHR

On June 23, 1956, Saskatoon's new city hall was officially opened, providing much needed space for an expanding civic administration. Here, demolition begins on the old city hall, the former King Edward School, which when purchased in 1910 was to be a temporary facility but served for over forty years. *Photo PH 2001-22 courtesy* SPL – LHR

The cenotaph, relocated from 21st Street and 2nd Avenue to the front of the new city hall was rededicated in October 1957. This was to be the site of annual Remembrance Day ceremonies as well as public gatherings and protests in years to come. *Photo LH 33 58 by the Saskatoon* StarPhoenix, *courtesy* SPL – LHR

Looking north over the western fringe of the city, ca. 1956. The Union Stockyards (far left) and the Hi-Way Royalite Refinery (Gulf Canada at the time of its demolition in the 1970s) were then on the north side of 11th Street West. The hangar building (right middle) housed the Western Development Museum until its move to the exhibition grounds in 1972. In the foreground are the Pion-Era grounds, the site of the annual show recalling early settlement on the prairies. This area is now part of the Gordie Howe Park recreational complex. *Photo B 5116 by Leonard Hillyard, courtesy* SPL – LHR

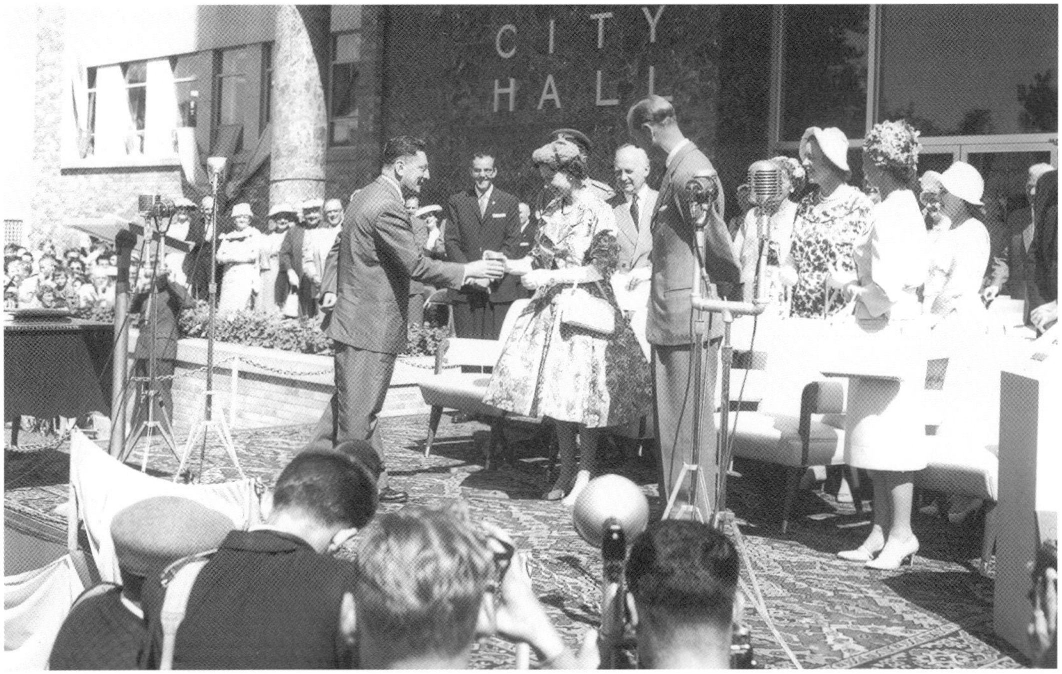

Mayor Sid Buckwold officially welcomed Her Majesty Queen Elizabeth and Prince Philip to Saskatoon and presented them with a jar of Saskatoon-berry jam during their royal visit to Canada in 1959. *Photo B 4924 by Leonard Hillyard, courtesy* SPL – LHR

In November 1956, the Temperance Colony House, one of the original houses in Saskatoon, was moved from 526 Main Street to the Pion-Era grounds on 11th Street West. It was moved to the exhibition grounds when the Western Development Museum moved there in 1972. It remained there until the mid 1980s when it was determined to be beyond repair and was demolished. *Photo S-Sp B 4593-1 courtesy Sask Archives,* StarPhoenix *Collection*

Looking west over Intercontinental Packers on 11th Street West in July 1959. Established in a former (1911) tractor factory (right middle) in 1940 by Fred Mendel, Intercon became a mainstay of the Saskatoon economy. Part of the Montgomery Place subdivision is visible in the upper right. The first twenty-five houses had been constructed in 1946. It was incorporated into the City of Saskatoon in 1955. *Photo B 51526 by Leonard Hillyard, courtesy SPL – LHR*

Squadron Commander Marion Graham (left front) and other members of the Women's Division (WDS), attached to the 406 Tactical Bomber Squadron, formed up in front of a B25 Mitchell bomber on their base at the Saskatoon airport, ca. 1953. The 406 Squadron was stationed in Saskatoon as part of the NATO Cold War defence system from 1947 until it was disbanded in 1964. *Photo courtesy Marion Graham*

In December 1955, passengers wait to board a plane in the new terminal building (inset), completed that spring by the Department of Transport at the Saskatoon Airport. *Photo S-SP-B 3414-4 courtesy Sask Archives; Photo B 14949 by Leonard Hillyard, courtesy SPL – LHR*

University students crowd Bell's restaurant (later Walling's) at College and Cumberland over lunchtime during the winter term in 1953. *Photo B 15097 by Leonard Hillyard, courtesy SPL – LHR*

An aerial view of the university campus in 1955. The University Hospital (left middle) had been completed and the Murray Memorial Library (centre) is under construction. However, temporary quarters such as the Hangar building, located where College Drive narrows (right middle), served for decades to come. The Town of Sutherland (centre background) amalgamated with the City of Saskatoon in 1956. In 1959, Saskatoon's city limits were expanded to include the university as well. *Photo courtesy University of Saskatchewan News Service Office*

The 1957 version of the Intensely Vigorous College Nine create quite a din as they are towed around the Bowl on campus. This loosely organized group, with changing numbers and personnel, already had a three-year tradition of entertaining fellow students and "townies" with their antics. The newly completed Murray Memorial Library is in the background. *Photo PH 96-177-16 by Murray Gibson, courtesy SPL – LHR*

Music professor Murray Adaskin (right) joins a group of students around a classroom piano on campus, ca. 1959. Roy Romanow, a future premier of Saskatchewan, stands behind the piano (far left). *Photo A 2146 courtesy U of S Archives*

Professor Murray Adaskin and a colleague show off the rare Amati string instruments that had been purchased by the University of Saskatchewan. In March 1959, local musicians gave the first public performance using the priceless instruments. *Photo S-SP-B 5279-1, courtesy Sask Archives,* StarPhoenix *Collection*

Looking west from Warman Road (foreground) over the northern margin of the city, ca. 1959. Forty-second Street (extending west from right centre) was designated as part of the planned Circle Drive bypass route. The Prairie Fibreboard plant (presently the site of the Rona Home Centre) produced building materials from pressed straw between 1956 and the early 1960s. *Photo PH 91-4-6 by James R. Teed, courtesy SPL – LHR*

Chapter Eight

1960-1969

In 1960 the Russians put a man in space; in 1969 the Americans landed one on the moon. The years in between were ones of staggering political, social, cultural, and technological innovation. Although marked by escalating global military tensions, the 1960s were nevertheless years of unbridled confidence. The future was here, and the people of Saskatoon raced to embrace it.

In 1960 the last steam-powered locomotive chuffed its way through Saskatoon. By the end of the decade, the electric trolley buses that had replaced the old streetcars were poised to also become things of the past. During the intervening ten years, transportation in Saskatoon underwent significant changes as the number of automobiles on city streets continued its dizzying upward spiral.

With the increasing number of automobiles came an ever more pressing need for more bridges and for a highway bypass system such as had been first proposed in the Yorath Plan of 1913. The original plan had been to build bridges on the north and south edges of the city, linked by the present-day Circle Drive. This project was shelved in favour of a downtown revitalization plan that would see the southern leg of Circle Drive veer north along the old CNR right of way and cross into downtown on what is now the Senator Sid Buckwold Bridge. Rather

Opposite page: Looking east over Saskatoon in 1960. Access to the central downtown area from the east side was restricted by the river, and from Riversdale (foreground) by the CNR yards. The increasing number of private vehicles going in and out of the downtown each day made traffic a major concern for residents and planners. *Photo QC 1618-12 by Gordon Skogland, courtesy SPL – LHR*

An auto carrier unable to pass under the 23rd Street subway from downtown is stopped cold, ca. 1963. *Photo QC 4141-1 courtesy* SPL – LHR

than channelling traffic around the city, Circle Drive would instead pipe it into its very heart.

The construction of the Idylwyld Freeway and removal of the rail yards from downtown was probably the crowning achievement of Mayor Sid Buckwold's ten years in office. The real estate that was freed up south of 22nd Street between 1st Avenue and Idylwyld became home to the Midtown Plaza shopping mall, a new YMCA building, and the Centennial Auditorium. With the rail yards gone, traffic could move between the eastern and western halves of the city with a freedom that had not been possible since almost before there were automobiles in Saskatoon.

Saskatoon's first experiment with a European-style traffic circle was built at 8th Street and Circle Drive in the late 1960s. Intended to allow the free flow of traffic at what was expected to become one of the city's busiest intersections, it was feared and detested by many of the city's drivers. Others – the more widely travelled perhaps, or those of a more adventurous frame of mind – seemed quite unaffected by it, and indeed there were those who professed to love it.

Development in the city's northern industrial districts reflected new economic opportunities in mining and industry, while the city's educational facilities were expanding with the construction of the Saskatchewan Technical Institute (now the Saskatchewan Institute of Applied Science and Technology's Kelsey Campus) and the addition of several new buildings at the University of Saskatchewan including the $1.75 million linear accelerator, which opened in 1964.

New residential construction was concentrated on the east side of the city, and included College Park, Brevoort Park, and Eastview, as well as the Massey Place and Westview subdivisions on the northwest edge of the city. In the downtown area, the Mendel Art Gallery was built in 1964 along the riverbank next to Kinsmen Park, while older residential areas in the downtown core were being invaded by highrise office towers and parkades as the demand for space intensified.

In the older parts of Saskatoon, urban renewal was the order of the day. For the city to meet its future potential, it would be necessary for it to cut the ties that bound it to the past. The downtown core felt the full weight of this rush to progress. As it was completely built up, no new construction could occur unless another building fell first. And fall they did. The elegant downtown library and the old Number 1 Fire Hall on 23rd Street were both demolished in 1966 to make way for a new library building. Other notable landmarks torn down included the Masonic Lodge at 404 21st Street East in 1962 and the Toronto General Trusts Building on 21st Street and 2nd Avenue the following year.

Other buildings were renovated to give them a more modern look. The stately King George Hotel was one of many downtown buildings given new facades and rooflines to mimic the uncluttered look of the new architectural styles. In 1968, city council even considered replacing the University Bridge after concerns were raised about its safety. The proposal was ultimately dropped in favour of much needed (and much cheaper) repairs to its decking. By the end of the decade, public concern for the preservation of buildings with architectural and historic merit was to become increasingly apparent, paving the way for the heritage movements of the 1970s.

Pedestrians use the "scramble corner" crosswalk at 21st Street and 2nd Avenue North in July 1960. Scramble corners were convenient for pedestrians on the wide streets of Saskatoon's downtown but did little to help the movement or parking of vehicles in the area. *Photo B 7937 by Leonard Hillyard, courtesy SPL – LHR*

Holiday Park in the city's far southwest was built over a number of years

Looking north over central Saskatoon in April 1966. The CN rail yards had been removed and the Idywyld Freeway Bridge (now Senator Sid Buckwold Bridge) and freeway are under construction along the former railway right of way. The A. L. Cole power station on the west river bank (centre) was taken out of service in 1983 and demolished in 1996. *Lumby Collection No. 67-5 courtesy Sask Archives*

beginning in 1960. By the end of the decade it featured a golf course, football and baseball facilities, an indoor skating rink, and a campground. The Western Development Museum (originally on 11th Street West at the north edge of the park) and Pion-Era exhibition had been integral to the early designs but were lost in the implementation, as was the Grand Prix racing track, steeplechase track, permanent midway, and boating lake. Holiday Park was renamed in honour of native son and hockey legend Gordie Howe in 1966.

The federal government's Forest Nursery Station north of Sutherland was transferred to the City of Saskatoon in 1966, and plans made to develop it for recreational purposes, including the opening of a municipal zoo in place of the privately owned Golden Gate Animal Park, then west of the city on 33rd Street.

It was a period of immense social awakening. The prosperity that had come to North America after the Second World War helped spawn a new socially conscious and politically aware youth culture, which, while it may have had its roots among the artists and intellectuals of the 1950s, had by the mid-sixties become a force all its own.

For many, it was the music that set the tone for the popular culture of the 1960s. The stylings of American artists such as Elvis Presley and Chuck Berry may have launched a new musical genre in the 1950s, but it was the British Invasion that provided the creative engine for popular music and pop culture as the 1960s progressed. Folk music, which had been undergoing a revival in North America for a number of years, also blossomed in the 1960s as the voice of popular protest of a generation increasingly aware of human rights, the environment, and international issues.

In Saskatoon, artists such as Joni Mitchell were a regular fixture at clubs like the Louis Riel, where she played her first paying gig on Hallowe'en night in 1962. Humphrey and the Dumptrucks was formed in Saskatoon in 1967 and acquired a dedicated following before hitting the big time with back-to-back recorded hits in the early 1970s.

In the late 1960s, women in Saskatoon were piling their hair high into bouffants and beehives. Mini-skirts over high, shiny white boots were "in," hot pants were "hot," and pantsuits were all the rage. If the hippie styles of San Francisco's Haight-Ashbury district had taken the rest of the world by storm, Saskatoon was still all Carnaby Street "mod." Regardless of the clothes they wore, however, the newest generation of Saskatonians to come of age was shaking itself free of the past in an orgy of experimental hairstyles, lifestyles, and political philosophies to equal that found anywhere else in North America.

Although the effects of the post-war baby boom continued to be felt, Saskatoon's population was beginning to age. The city's population jumped from about 90,000 in 1960 to 129,000 in 1969. But while the number of students enrolled at the University of Saskatchewan and in the city's high schools more than doubled during the 1960s, the number attending the city's elementary schools increased by only about 50 per cent during the same period, and had in fact begun to decline by 1969. The baby boom, it appeared, was over. The decade that added the phrase "generation gap" to the English language was coming to a close, and the youth of the 1960s were set to become the adults of the 1970s.

By 1969 the construction of the CN Tower (at 21st Street and 1st Avenue) was well under way. The CN railway station and adjoining railway buildings were demolished soon after with the opening of the new station at Chappell Yards on the southwest edge of the city. *Photo B 11569 by Leonard Hillyard, courtesy SPL – LHR*

The old city market building in Market Square at Avenue A was about to be demolished in the spring of 1963. It had been the site of political protests as well as the farmers' market and auctions over the years. No. 1 Fire Hall was constructed on the site in 1964. *Photo LH 2023 courtesy* SPL – LHR

Fred Mendel with his family at a reception following the 1964 opening of the Mendel Art Gallery and Civic Conservatory on the riverbank opposite Kinsmen Park. Mendel had made a major contribution to its construction and donated paintings from his own collection to the gallery. *Photo S-SP-5871-2 courtesy Sask Archives* StarPhoenix *Collection*

The interior of the new public library, constructed on the site of the old No. 1 Fire Hall and library on 23rd Street, is visible through its large front windows on an evening not long after its opening in 1965. *Photo LH 2505 by Lumby Productions, courtesy* SPL – LHR

The newly opened Holiday Park municipal golf course in 1962. It was part of the Holiday Park (now Gordie Howe Park) recreational complex, which also included a trailer court, ball diamonds, and football bowl. *Photo LH 4460C by Leonard Hillyard, courtesy* SPL – LHR

Denny Carr, co-host of the popular *Wal n' Den Show* on CFQC Radio, reports from Mayfair Pool in the summer of 1965. *Photo 91-55-344 by CFQC staff, courtesy SPL – LHR*

Looking northwest in the fall of 1960, over Grosvenor Park on the city's east side. It was the first neighbourhood designed by the city's new planning department in 1954. In the foreground is Grosvenor Park Shopping Centre, one of the first suburban malls in the city, located on the newly widened 8th Street East (left foreground), which provided a major artery into the city from the east. *Photo B 7558 by Leonard Hillyard, courtesy SPL – LHR*

Looking east over the north central part of the city, ca. 1960. Caswell Hill is in the foreground. The H-huts of the former No. 7 Flying School at Avenue A (Idywyld Drive) and 33rd Street West, housing the Community Apartments, Provincial Geriatric Centre, and Provincial Vocational Training School, were cleared in 1963 for the Central Saskatchewan Technical Institute (now SIAST Kelsey Campus) that now occupies the site. The Saskatchewan Wheat Pool and Robin Hood flour mills are in the centre. *Photo QC 1618-11 by Gordon Skogland, courtesy SPL – LHR*

Looking north over the Starlight Drive-In theatre at 8th Street East and Preston Avenue, ca. 1965. It was the first drive-in in Saskatchewan when it was built in 1950, then just outside the city limits. It was demolished in 1968 and replaced by Sherwood Chevrolet. After that moved to Circle Drive in 2003, several retail outlets, including Winners and London Drugs, were built there. *Photo courtesy Les Howard*

Soapbox race cars lined up to compete in timed heats on Bedford Road, ca. 1960. The soapbox derby was a popular summer event sponsored by the Playgrounds Association for a number of years. *Photo QC 1207 by* CFQC *staff, courtesy* SPL – LHR

A blindfolded boy scout makes the draw for the Kinsmen car draw on the grandstand stage during the exhibition in July 1960. *Photo B 7849 by Leonard Hillyard, courtesy* SPL – LHR

Looking northeast in 1968 over the controversial traffic circle at 8th Street and Circle Drive. The newly opened Evan Hardy Collegiate (centre back) would become part of College Park subdivision. A travel-trailer dealership and JD's Restaurant occupy the site of the present-day Circle Park Mall. *Photo CP 68-19-2 by Creative Professional Photographers, courtesy* SPL – LHR

A staff party in Labatt's Gardens on the river bank behind Labatt's Brewery (formerly the Saskatoon Brewing Company) in July 1961. These grounds, now the Fred Mitchell Memorial Gardens, have been maintained since the demolition of the brewery in 1993 and are still a popular setting for picnics and wedding photos. *Photo B 9208 courtesy* SPL – LHR

The miniature train and merry-go-round, built by the Kinsmen in Kinsmen Park during the 1950s, were popular attractions for children in the mid 1960s. The playground, including a new train and merry-go-round, was rebuilt in the 1980s. *Photo QC 3478-4 courtesy* SPL – LHR

Helen Hase Lumby hosted *Miss Helen's Kindergarten,* a popular weekday-morning children's program on CFQC-TV in the 1960s. *Photo QC 1875-2 courtesy* SPL – LHR

Joni Mitchell, a rising international folksinger and songwriter, with host Verne Prior on *Top of the Clock* in March 1969, when she returned to Saskatoon for a performance at the Centennial Auditorium. A graduate of Aden Bowman Collegiate, Mitchell often demonstrated her talents at the Louis Riel coffee house, a popular hangout for university students on Broadway in the early 1960s. *Photo QC 4646-1 courtesy* SPL – LHR

CFQC-TV coverage of the 1963 federal election: (l to r) Les Edwards of CFQC News, host Greg Barnsley, and commentator Norman Ward, a political scientist at the University of Saskatchewan. *Photo QC 2448-8 courtesy* SPL – LHR

The Gordie Brandt Trio, consisting of (left to right) Barney Kutz, "Buddy" Rodgers, and Gordie Brandt, made regular appearances on CFQC-TV in the early 1960s. Here they appear with host Stan Thomas. *Photo QC 890-1 courtesy* SPL – LHR

A civil defence siren on top of Haultain School in Nutana, ca. 1966, to warn of possible nuclear attack or local emergencies. Some houses built in Saskatoon during the Cold War had fallout shelters in the basement. The School for the Deaf (R.J.D. Williams Building) on Cumberland is seen in the centre background. *Photo QC 1979-1 courtesy* SPL – LHR

An antiwar protest march heads across the University Bridge from the university to city hall in the fall of 1962. The Cold War and the possibility of a nuclear conflict between the superpowers was very real in the 1960s. *Photo S-SP - B 2724-3 courtesy Sask Archives* StarPhoenix *Collection*

Dr. Marc Baltzan (right foreground) and associates at a news conference following their first successful kidney transplant, the second in Canada, at the University Hospital in February 1964. *Photo QC 4118-5 courtesy SPL – LHR*

Bernie Blanchette received the Saskatoon Blades most valuable player award in front of the timekeeper's box in the Saskatoon Arena during one of the last games of the 1967-68 season. The Blades replaced the Junior Quakers as the Saskatoon franchise in the Saskatchewan Junior Hockey League in 1964, then joined the Western Canada Hockey League (now the Western Hockey League) when it was formed two years later. *Photo QC 4360-1 courtesy* SPL – LHR

Recreational skating on a Sunday afternoon at Rutherford Rink in January 1964. Rutherford was the site of regular intramural hockey games as well as the home of the Huskies hockey club that competed in the Canadian Intercollegiate Athletics Union (CIAU). *Photo A 1055 courtesy U of S Archives*

A track meet at Griffiths Stadium at College Drive and Cumberland Avenue opposite the university campus, ca. 1963. The field was moved to its present location when College Drive was widened and realigned in 1965. *Photo A 3409 courtesy U of S Archives*

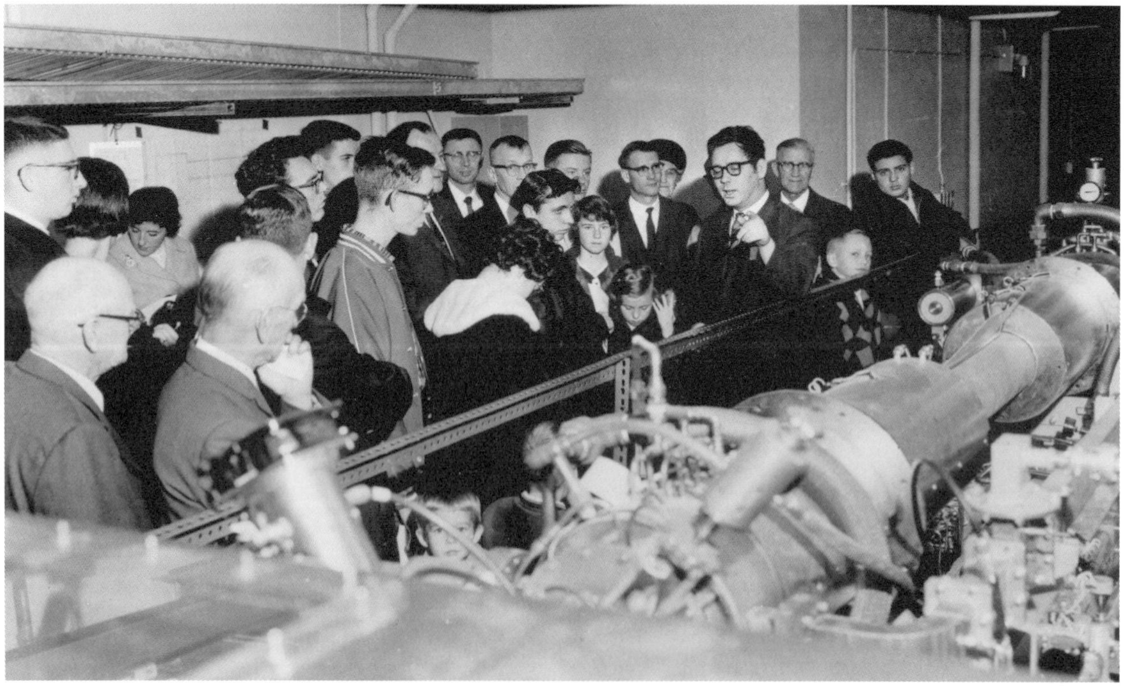

Visitors at the opening of the linear accelerator on campus in 1966. *Photo A-8643 courtesy U of S Archives*

Saskatoon Merchants catcher George Lacoursiere watches a fly ball to left field in a game against the Windsor Taverns, who represented Ontario in the National Senior Men's Fastball Championship held at the Gordie Howe Park recreational complex in the fall of 1969. The Merchants went on to win their first national championship trophy in this tournament. The Saskatoon Imperials won the 1969 Canadian Senior Women's Fastball Championship as well. Both the Merchants and Imperials were installed in the Saskatchewan Sports Hall of Fame in 1984. *Photo QC 4865-13 courtesy* SPL – LHR

Looking north over the Dominion Forest Nursery Station – the Forestry Farm – north of Sutherland in the fall of 1962. It was turned over to the City of Saskatoon in 1966, and a zoo was established in 1973 when the city purchased the animals of the Golden Gate Animal Park (then on 33rd Street West). *Photo LH 9490 courtesy* SPL – LHR

A protest rally organized by the National Farmers Union in front of the Bessborough, where Prime Minister Trudeau was staying during a brief visit to Saskatoon in July 1969. A load of spoiled wheat was dumped in the street to protest the lack of federal government support in marketing prairie grain. *Photo CP 5717-23 Creative Professional Photographers collection, courtesy* SPL – LHR

LOANS
GAC
Coca-Cola
STERLING SHOPS
Sally's
THE BANK OF NOVA SCOTIA
Canada Trust
21st ST E

Chapter Nine
1970-1979

Here, as elsewhere, political and social forces that had begun to take shape in the 1960s continued to gather momentum through the 1970s. Events in places far removed from Saskatoon and brought to our homes by the magic of television continued to have an impact on our daily lives. In Canada, martial law was declared during the 1970 October Crisis in which members of a Quebec separatist group kidnapped and murdered a Quebec politician. From the Middle East to Biafra and from Ireland to South East Asia, the world was wracked with war, murder, famine, and upheaval. In 1973 the price of oil suddenly quadrupled, with economic and political consequences that continue to reverberate today.

The hippie culture of the 1960s reached its full extent in Saskatoon in the early 1970s, to the alarm and dismay of local parents, police, and politicians. But the youth movement of the previous decade was gradually changing into something a little less threatening, a little more "normal," and this trend showed up in Saskatoon too. By the mid-1970s Flower Power had turned into the Me Generation, polyester had replaced sandals and beads as the uniform of choice, and disco music ruled the radio.

Opposite page: Looking north on 2nd Avenue, ca. 1973, the former core of the city's central business district. In 1978, all the buildings from the Bank of Nova Scotia and the Capitol Theatre to the corner at 22nd Street (left middle) were torn down to make way for the Scotia Centre and Scotiabank. In the right background is the overhead walkway constructed in the 1960s from the Hudson's Bay department store at 23rd Street to its parkade across the street. The walkway and parkade were demolished in 2004. *Photo LH 5108 courtesy SPL – LHR*

Paddlers haul their canoes up the bank on July 13, 1970, after finishing the river portion of the Louis Riel relay race. Horseback riders and runners covered the other portions, which took place along the river banks. This race was a key attraction of Louis Riel Day, sponsored by CFQC-TV, a Sunday afternoon of festivities on the downtown river bank each summer from 1968 to 1999. *Photo S-SP-A 6146-25 courtesy Sask Archives* StarPhoenix *Collection*

There was also a ferment of activity in music, the arts, theatre, and culture in Saskatoon during the 1970s: the birth of the Sundog Arts & Crafts Faire, and the flowering of our own Left Bank, the Ritz Hotel's somewhat seedy Apollo Room. Interesting little art galleries featuring the work of local artists increased in popularity. The annual Louis Riel Day race attracted thousands of people to the city's riverbank parks. Although live theatre had long been a staple of the social scene in Saskatoon, it gained particular prominence with the establishment of such professional companies as Persephone and 25th Street theatres, among others. Opera in Saskatoon received a boost with the founding of the Saskatoon Opera Association in 1978. The Saskatoon Symphony Orchestra (founded in 1927), live jazz and folk music, and dance were also well supported by the people of Saskatoon during the 1970s.

The 1970s also witnessed a surge of community activism and grassroots political involvement within the city. Community and neighbourhood associations acted as forums for people anxious to see that their vision of what the city should look like became part of the public debate. Popular opposition to a proposed uranium refinery in Warman and the demolition of the Capitol Theatre, and a general concern for the urban environment, were critical to the formation of influential community groups such as the Saskatoon Environmental Society, the Saskatoon Heritage Society, and perhaps most importantly, the Meewasin Valley Authority, which was given stewardship over the Saskatchewan River where it wound its way through the city.

Saskatoon's downtown skyline changed dramatically during the 1970s, beginning with the official opening of the Midtown Plaza and CN Tower on July 30, 1970. Core area merchants eyed the new mall warily, hoping on the one hand that it would help bring customers back to downtown and away from the new suburban shopping centres, and worried on the other that it would also draw them away from their own businesses. The 21st Street parking mall between 1st and 4th Avenues owes its creation to their own brand of community activism. At the same time, the construction of new glass-and-steel office buildings and residential high-rises was rapidly changing the look and feel Saskatoon's downtown. A new police building replaced the by-now cramped quarters in the old Municipal

Justice Building, kitty-corner from city hall, and provincial government offices in Saskatoon moved into the grandly futuristic Sturdy Stone Building on the site of the boom-era Standard Trust building at 3rd Avenue North and 22nd Street. The Sheraton Cavalier Hotel went up across from the Bessborough (and was joined to it by a tunnel under Spadina Crescent). A number of older buildings were also given facelifts to give them a more contemporary look, a continuation of a process that had begun in the 1960s.

The city's transport capabilities were expanded with the opening of a new airport terminal and a much-needed new Saskatchewan Transportation Company bus depot. New industrial development and a state-of-the-art sewage treatment plant were built in the city's north end. New buildings also went up at the university including a new students' centre and a separate building for the College of Dentistry (originally in the Health Sciences Building), among others. University Hospital got a new parkade and construction began on the Diefenbaker Centre. The city's highway entrances continued to see a proliferation of shopping centres, motels, and fast-food outlets.

Saskatoon's population continued to increase, although in nowhere near the same proportions as the baby boom years of the 1950s and 1960s. The decline in elementary school enrolment that had begun in the late 1960s continued. High school enrolments stayed pretty much the same throughout the decade, while enrolment at the university grew only marginally. Nevertheless, through natural increase and in-migration (primarily from rural Saskatchewan), the city's population grew to 148,000 by the end of 1979.

The 1970s were good years for the construction industry in Saskatoon, with building permits issued by the city showing a steady increase (both in numbers and overall value) throughout the decade. Residential development during the 1970s was greatest along the city's western and northwestern fringe. Older neighbourhoods like Massey Place and Meadowgreen were extended farther west, and new ones such as Confederation Heights, Fairhaven, Pacific Heights, and Parkridge were begun. On the north side, residential development also began to fill the space between the river and Warman Road with the construction of the new River Heights and Lawson Heights subdivisions. At the eastern end of 8th Street, development was

The Midtown Plaza officially opened on July 30, 1970. It provided a new commercial area in downtown Saskatoon and offered underground as well as surface parking. The Centennial Auditorium (right middle) on 22nd Street would also draw people to the expanded downtown. *Photo CP - 70-24 courtesy SPL – LHR*

Opposite Midtown Plaza, the former Massey-Harris warehouse at 1st Avenue and 22nd Street was demolished in 1973. The Saskatchewan Regional Community College and the Department of Social Services had occupied it for a time after Massey-Harris left in 1969. It was replaced by the Holiday Inn in 1974, later renamed the Quality Inn and now the Saskatoon Hilton Garden Inn. *Photo courtesy William P. Delainey*

happening in East College Park and Wildwood, as well as farther south in Lakeview. Altogether, some 20,000 homes were built during the years 1971 to 1980.

With prosperity came an increased demand for leisure activities. The federal government launched its Participaction fitness program in 1971 with a series of television commercials unfavourably comparing the fitness level of the average thirty-year-old Canadian to that of the average sixty-year-old Swede. Locally, major sporting events began and ended the decade: the Canada Winter Games in 1971 and the Western Canada Summer Games in 1979. With a distinct dearth of mountainous terrain in the vicinity on which to hold alpine ski events, organizers of the Canada Winter Games built one from scratch, piling an entire mountain's worth of dirt and fill on the edge of Blackstrap Coulee, a shallow valley south of the city. Mount Blackstrap opened just in the nick of time, on December 15, 1970, only two months before the games were scheduled to begin.

Other, much less ambitious sports facilities were built during the 1970s,

On December 15, 1970, world ski champion Nancy Greene Raine (centre) opened Mount Blackstrap. This artificial hill was constructed for the Canada Winter Games, held in Saskatoon in 1971. *Photo S-SP - B6302-4 courtesy Sask. Archives*

including the Harry Bailey Aquatic Centre (Saskatoon's first indoor swimming pool), the Cosmo Civic Centre, the Saskatoon Field House, and the ACT Arena. One city sporting landmark that did not survive the decade was the old ski jump on the east river bank near the CPR bridge at 33rd Street. Long since fallen out of use, it was declared a danger and pulled down in 1978.

The new Western Development Museum opened next to the exhibition grounds in 1972. Saskatoon finally got its second TV station – the CBC – in 1972. The addition of three new FM radio stations and the introduction of cable television in the late 1970s ushered in a whole new entertainment era for Saskatonians. Other notable firsts and lasts for the decade included the hiring of the first female police recruit for Saskatoon in 1973, the last electric trolley bus run on May 10, 1974, and the last tuberculosis patient being discharged from the Saskatoon Sanatorium in 1978.

Marjorie Dressyman from the Red Pheasant Reserve greets Prime Minister Trudeau during a reception in Exhibition Stadium following the opening ceremonies (February 12th) of the 1971 Canada Winter Games. Facing them is Allan Sapp, a renowned artist also from the Red Pheasant Reserve. *Photo CP 6128 courtesy SPL – LHR*

For all the turmoil in the world, a continued flowering of the arts and culture, reasonably good economic growth, and an overall sense of well-being ensured that the quality of life here remained high. The little city by the river had seen some tumultuous times in the years since the end of the Second World War, and it was now time for the people of Saskatoon to sit back and enjoy the fruits of prosperity while they lasted.

High school teams in the city finals of *Reach for the Top* at the CFQC-TV studios in the spring of 1971. City Park went on to represent Saskatchewan at the national final in Halifax. *Reach for the Top* was moved to the new CBC station, CBKST, established in Saskatoon in 1972 when CFQC-TV became a CTV affiliate. *Photo QC 5134-4 courtesy SPL – LHR*

Competitors on the driving range of the Saskatoon Golf and Country Club during a CPGA tournament held there in August 1971. The new Marquis Downs horseracing track, completed in 1969 on the adjacent exhibition grounds, is visible in the background. *Photo S-SP - A 6509-6 courtesy Sask Archives* StarPhoenix *Collection*

Looking south over the Diamond Intersection at 33rd Street and Warman Road/1st Avenue just before it was reconstructed in 1972 to provide better access to downtown from the north. *Photo S-SP - 7204-28 courtesy Sask Archives* StarPhoenix *Collection*

Members of the Intensely Vigorous College Nine entertain University of Saskatchewan president J. W. T. Spinks and his guest, Nobel Laureate Gerhard Herzberg, in the cafeteria of Marquis Hall, ca. 1972. *Photo A-4806 courtesy U of S Archives*

"Boomtown" main street under construction in the new Western Development Museum on the exhibition grounds in February 1972. *Photo S-SP - B 7063-4 courtesy Sask Archives* StarPhoenix *Collection*

Workers picket this construction site at the Union Centre on the west edge of the city in July 1972. Interruptions in the construction and service industries occurred frequently in Saskatoon during the 1970s, a period of abnormally high inflation. Photo S-SP - A 7164-3 courtesy Sask Archives StarPhoenix *Collection*

Looking east along the new 22nd Street entrance to the city, ca. 1973. Space was left for an interchange where 22nd Street West intersected with Circle Drive. It was finally constructed in 2004. The Union Centre at 3311 Fairlight Drive is shown in the right foreground. Underground services to the Confederation Park Shopping Centre, then under construction, are being installed (left foreground). *Photo S-SP - B 7203-2 courtesy Sask Archives* StarPhoenix *Collection*

The last of Saskatoon's trolley buses, which had been taken out of service in May 1974, were shipped to Vancouver, where they were put back into service. Despite the sharp rise in petroleum prices in the early 1970s, Saskatoon Transit believed that diesel buses could more efficiently serve the expanding residential areas of the city. *Photo courtesy William A. S. Sarjeant*

The Mendel Art Gallery and Conservatory in its river-bank setting on Spadina Crescent during the summer of 1974. *Photo HST-013 courtesy City of Saskatoon Archives*

The parking lot of Market Mall on the southeast side of Saskatoon after a heavy thunderstorm flooded many low-lying areas on May 26, 1974. The McEown Tower high-rise apartment (left) and the Saskatchewan Teachers' Federation (right) are in the background *Photo LH 3677 courtesy* SPL – LHR

Adilman's at Avenue B and 20th Street West was the anchor of the Riversdale retail area, and the only locally owned department store in Saskatoon in 1974. Adilman's closed in 1975 after more than fifty years at that location. A variety of businesses have occupied the building since.*Photo PH 97-40-1 courtesy* SPL – LHR

Members of the Saskatoon Chile Support Committee picket on 2nd Avenue South in June 1977 to protest the 1973 coup that toppled the democratically-elected government in Chile. *Photo S-SP - A 7539-3 courtesy Sask Archives* StarPhoenix *Collection*

The Apollo Room at the Ritz Hotel, shown here in the 1970s, celebrated the historic Apollo 11 moon landing of 1969, but the real attraction was its clientele: artists, actors, musicians, craftspeople, university students and professors, social activists, and denizens of the hippie culture. Located on 21st Street between 1st and 2nd Avenues in what had been James Clinkskill's store and later the Bijou Theatre, the Ritz Hotel was demolished in the mid 1980s. *Photo PH 2000-74-3 by Bill Steeves, Creative Professional Photographers collection, courtesy SPL – LHR*

Local artists, ca. 1974, kibitz inside the door of the Avenue Building on 3rd Avenue South, where the Shoestring Gallery was located: (l to r, back) Jane Evans, Warren Brownridge, Marlene Zora, Elyse St. George, Jerry Didur, Lorna Cutting; (front) Rebecca Wilson, Jo Shepherd, Ann Newdigate Mills. The Shoestring Gallery was established in 1971 as a local artists' cooperative. In 1982 it became part of the A.K.A. Gallery. *Photo PH 89-113-2 courtesy SPL – LHR*

Persephone Theatre's production of "Cruel Tears" in March 1975. Written by Ken Mitchell, this prairie "opera" included music by Humphrey and the Dumptrucks, a popular local bluegrass band. Persephone Theatre was founded in 1974. After occupying various temporary venues, it moved into its own quarters in a remodelled church on Rusholme Road in 1981. *Photo PH 91-50-1 courtesy SPL – LHR*

The Saskatoon Women's Calendar Collective produced the 1976 issue of *Herstory* to celebrate the achievements of Canadian women: (clockwise from bottom) Dorothy Hudec, Beth Foster, Erin Shoemaker, Muriel Wiens, Pam Baxter, Joanne Fink, and Candace Savage. Founded in 1975 (International Women's Year), this locally-produced calendar now has a national market. *Photo MG 133 courtesy U of S Archives*

Looking north on 5th Avenue from 22nd Street East in 1976. High-rise apartment buildings replaced many single-family houses that had occupied the eastern margin of downtown. *Photo LH 5224 courtesy* SPL – LHR

Regent's Auto Service (since demolished) at 316 Idywyld North was one of the few Spanish-style service stations of the pre-Second World War era remaining in Saskatoon by 1976. The Rumely Building (centre background), constructed in 1912 as a farm machinery warehouse in the former CNR industrial area, was occupied by Brown's furniture wholesale and auction centre. *Photo courtesy William A. S. Sarjeant*

Fitness instructors practise routines during a 1976 clinic in the YMCA building, which had been constructed five years earlier next to the Centennial Auditorium. "Participaction," a fitness campaign that included a competition with the citizens of Umea, Sweden, encouraged Saskatonians to get fit. *Photo S-SP A 9069 courtesy Sask Archives* StarPhoenix *Collection*

A school meet on the Clarence Downey Speed Skating Oval behind the new Cairns Field baseball diamond in Gordie Howe Park in January 1976. Constructed for the Canada Winter Games in Saskatoon in 1971, the oval is the home of the Lions' Speed Skating Club and the site of annual speed-skating meets. *Photo S-SP A 9102 courtesy Sask Archives* StarPhoenix *Collection*

Caren Rathie and Rob Reindl, local athletes and members of the Riversdale Track Club and the Saskatchewan track team, pose with Saskie, the mascot for the Western Canada Summer Games in Saskatoon in 1979. The Field House, built just east of Griffiths Stadium on the university campus, is a lasting legacy of the 1979 games. *Photo LH 5342 courtesy* SPL – LHR

Premier Allan Blakeney addresses a special convocation held during the national conference of Learned Societies at the University of Saskatchewan in the spring of 1979. To his right are University Chancellor J. G. Diefenbaker and University President Dr. Robert W. Begg. *Photo A-6611 courtesy U of S Archives*

A sprint to the finish on the portable wood track in the Saskatoon Arena rink during a university-sponsored Sled Dog track meet, ca. 1976. The announcers (left middle) were Dale Yellowlees and Paul Hack. This portable track, designed and built locally, was used for some thirty meets, including the annual Knights of Columbus international meets, held in the arena between 1965 and 1979. *Photo S-SP A 7432 courtesy Sask Archives* StarPhoenix *Collection*

Chapter Ten

1980-1989

The 1980s began with a bang. The 1970s had generally been good to the city, and the people of Saskatoon rang in the new decade with a feeling of continuing optimism. Some of that optimism was justified. Some was not, and for many the 1980s were a decade of dreams deferred. Drought wreaked havoc on farm incomes in the province, accelerating the depopulation of rural areas and exacerbating the effects of a recession that saw interest rates and unemployment levels (particularly for young people) go through the roof. The last of the baby boom generation came of age in the mid-1980s. Looking about them in this era of declining opportunities, they may well have viewed the future with a certain apprehension.

But the 1980s were also a decade of festivals and anniversaries in Saskatoon. In 1980 the city helped "Celebrate Saskatchewan" during the province's seventy-fifth birthday, followed in 1982 by the gala "Century Saskatoon," a year-long event commemorating the founding of Saskatoon by the Temperance Colonization Society in 1882. The University of Saskatchewan celebrated its seventy-fifth

Opposite page: Looking south along Warman Road toward downtown in the summer of 1980: the Lawson Heights Mall (foreground), Woodlawn Cemetery and part of the expanding north industrial area (right middle), and the easement reserved for the Circle Drive extension of 42nd Street, between the Lawson Heights and River Heights subdivisions (right middle). *Photo CP 8134 by Creative Professional Photographers, courtesy SPL – LHR*

Courtney Brown of the Winnipeg Assiniboia Club breaks the Canadian midget 50-metre record on December 31, 1980 at the Knights of Columbus Games. This was the first major track and field meet held in the new Field House. The Saskatoon Sports Hall of Fame has been located in the Field House since 1987. *Photo S-SP 80-12 courtesy Sask Archives* StarPhoenix *Collection*

anniversary the same year, as did Saskatoon's City Hospital – the first municipally owned hospital in Western Canada – two years later. In 1985, the city commemorated the hundredth anniversary of the Northwest Resistance, memorializing the event with a life-sized bronze statue of Gabriel Dumont on horseback. The best year for birthdays was 1989, when the Western Development Museum turned forty, the Mendel Art Gallery turned twenty-five, and the Meewasin Valley Authority turned ten.

The Meewasin Valley Authority held its first Winterfest in 1982, featuring traditional winter sports and the ritual burning of Christmas trees. The Sundog Arts & Crafts Faire was supplemented by the more upmarket Artisans' Craft Market, which omitted Sundog's festival element. Louis Riel Day continued to be a feature of the city's summer schedule. Folkfest, a three-day celebration of the city's multicultural heritage, began in 1980.

The recession of the early 1980s was caused for the most part by federal policies designed to control inflation. The economic life of the city carried on despite it all, with new buildings in a variety of architectural styles going up downtown, through the city's northern industrial area, and in the new research park north of the university campus. On campus at least fifteen new buildings or additions were constructed in the 1980s. The Diefenbaker Centre was completed as was the final phase of Place Riel, the new students' centre. Downtown, new highrises pierced the city's formerly modest silhouette, and glass-faced buildings rose like giant mirrored crystals to reflect their urban surroundings. New civic facilities built during the 1980s included a substantial addition to city hall, as well as the Lakewood and Lawson Civic Centres, which along with the Cosmo Civic Centre (built in 1977) combined branch libraries, swimming pools, and other facilities under one roof.

In the 1980s the trend toward sprawling indoor shopping malls continued with the Mall at Lawson Heights, which opened in October 1980 and was significantly expanded in 1989. The County Fair Plaza, which had been built at 8th Street and Acadia Drive in the late 1970s, was extended in the mid-eighties and became the Circle Park Mall. Later it was twinned with the Wildwood Mall across Acadia Drive by an underground link.

As new buildings went up, old ones came down. The Municipal Justice Building (the former police station) was demolished to make way for police parking. A new YWCA building and a highrise apartment tower went up on the site of King Edward School on 25th Street, which had been damaged by fire in 1979 and was subsequently demolished. The Saskatoon Arena on 19th Street – built during the height of the Depression in 1937 – closed in 1988 and was torn down the following year, as was the Saskatoon Sanatorium at the foot of Avenue K overlooking the river.

The city's population grew from 148,000 in 1980 to 184,000 in 1989, finally surpassing Regina as the province's largest city. While natural increase accounted for some of this growth, it was mostly at the expense of rural Saskatchewan. Demographically, the city had reached a plateau. Enrolment at Saskatoon's post-secondary institutions increased substantially during the 1980s, at least partly because of the lack of worthwhile career opportunities.

Poor economic conditions and high interest rates did not deter home

Looking west over downtown in the winter of 1981 when a major addition was being made to city hall (left foreground). The microwave tower atop the SaskTel building on 1st Avenue North is visible in the background. *SP file photo courtesy StarPhoenix*

In February 1981, the last remnant of the lobby of the Capitol Theatre was about to be torn down, making way for construction of the present Scotia Centre. The demolition of the Capitol fuelled a growing heritage movement in Saskatoon. *Photo CP 8254 courtesy SPL – LHR*

buyers, however. Between 1981 and 1990, nearly 17,000 houses were built in Saskatoon, mostly in the far southeast as well as in the north, primarily in Silverwood and Lawson Heights, and on the city's western fringe in Parkridge and Dundonald.

Construction of Saskatoon's Circle Drive continued throughout the decade. In 1983, the long-awaited Circle Drive Bridge opened in northern Saskatoon, connecting the city's east side with the new residential and industrial neighbourhoods in the city's north end. The traffic circle at 8th Street and Circle Drive – Saskatoon's most dangerous intersection – was dismantled in the summer of 1988 and replaced with traffic lights.

The number of riders on city buses reached its highest levels ever during the first half of the decade. Downtown, the 23rd Street transit terminal opened amidst much hoopla in November 1984. Later, as businesses folded on 23rd Street and the bus mall began attracting panhandlers, loiterers, and revellers from nearby bars, businesspeople and bus patrons were to question the wisdom of this move.

The VCR was to the 1980s what television had been to the 1950s. Initially a high-priced toy, the cost of a home video player dropped steadily until by the end of the decade renting a movie had become the single most popular leisure-time activity going. Operators of movie theatres, awash in red ink, responded by subdividing their theatres into multiple auditoriums and enticing audiences with "Two-Dollar Tuesdays" and second-run movies at reduced prices. Unable to compete in the new market, older theatres either shut down, or – like the Broadway Theatre, which began offering foreign and alternative films and live theatre – reinvented themselves.

Local sports continued to thrive. In 1982, outspoken Saskatoon booster Bill Hunter and former mayor Cliff Wright trekked to New York in an unsuccessful attempt to move the NHL's St. Louis Blues to Saskatoon. They were not able to convince the league that Saskatchewan could support an NHL franchise and the idea died. Saskatoon did get a new arena, however, as Saskatchewan Place (now the Credit Union Centre) officially opened in 1988, replacing the old Saskatoon Arena as the home of the Blades and the preferred venue for big-name entertainers in Saskatoon. In 1989 the city hosted the Labatt Brier Canadian men's curling championship, and in August of that year the 1989 Jeux Canada Games were held in Saskatoon.

The 1980s were also a time of protest and civil unrest. Citizens took democracy to the streets, marching in protest against government policy, high university tuition fees, nuclear energy, free trade, and an assortment of other grievances. Labour unrest was also in the news, particularly in the late 1980s when the University of Saskatchewan Faculty Association held its first ever full strike in the spring of 1988 and was legislated back to work after two weeks on the picket line. Postal workers and nurses were also out on strike that year, and in the fall of 1989 SIAST instructors walked out in a strike that lasted until well into the next year.

Federal government employees in Saskatoon rallied at the Vimy Memorial Bandstand in Kiwanis Park in the summer of 1980 to show support for workers across the country in ongoing contract negotiations. Labour demonstrations occurred quite frequently in Saskatoon during the 1980s. *Photo CP 8115-1 courtesy SPL – LHR*

It was a time of many contradictions. By the end of the decade, the flagging downtown business economy reflected a larger economic decline. Continuing drought conditions and poor crops helped dampen urban commerce as interest rates stayed high. By the end of the decade, unemployment had dropped slightly but remained well above 1970s levels. Nevertheless, the city had grown significantly. The number and value of building permits recorded by the City of Saskatoon remained high throughout the 1980s, and the number of housing starts was second only to the record-high levels of the 1970s. Yet this was also the same decade that the term "food bank" entered the public vocabulary. Once again, conditions in the city were dictated by forces and events beyond the control of local initiatives. Once again, Saskatoon and its people would simply have to make the best of what they had, and wait for better times to come again.

The former Schrader house at 321 6th Avenue North survives amid high-rise apartment blocks that tower over it, ca. 1981. It is one of the few single-family dwellings remaining in the downtown area. Its owner, lawyer Sy Halyk, chose to have it retrofitted as a legal office rather than replace it with a new building. The Saskatoon Heritage Society and the city's Municipal Heritage Advisory Committee applauded this decision. *Photo LH 4181 by John Duerkop, courtesy SPL – LHR*

A heavy thunderstorm flooded the Idywyld Drive underpass at 42nd Street on June 24, 1983. A young woman drowned in her car and millions of dollars of damage was done, particularly in the north part of the city, including the collapse of the roofs of Safeway in the Lawson Heights Mall and the new Modern Press (Western Producer) building on Millar Avenue. *Photo LH 4758 courtesy* SPL – LHR

Unemployed workers marched down 20th Street East on the way to a rally at the band shell in Kiwanis Park in the spring of 1983. *Photo S-SP A 20240-12 courtesy Sask Archives* StarPhoenix *Collection*

The official opening of Circle Drive Bridge on July 1, 1983. This bridge completed Circle Drive around the north end of the city, stimulating commercial and industrial growth in that area. *Photo LH 4761 courtesy* SPL – LHR

In the spring of 1983, players on the University of Saskatchewan Huskies hockey club carried coach Dave King in a triumphal skate around the ice. They had just won the Canadian Intercollegiate Hockey Championship in Moncton, NB. *Photo A-4369 courtesy U of S Archives*

A touring "funny car" dragster heads down the track at the Saskatoon International Raceway (now Saskatchewan International Raceway) south of the city, ca. 1983. SIR was constructed as the Southwinds International Raceway in 1966. The first car down the strip was the Midwest Auto dragster driven by Ken Achs. *Photo courtesy Les Howard*

Wendel Clark of the Saskatoon Blades drives down the left wing, avoiding a Prince Albert Raider check, in a WHL game in the Saskatoon Arena on 19th Street during the 1984-85 season. The Blades, like others in the city, were looking forward to a larger, modern multi-purpose complex to be built in the northwest fringe of Saskatoon. *Photo courtesy Saskatoon Blades Hockey Club*

In November 1984, Mayor Cliff Wright officially opened the new Saskatoon Transit bus mall on 23rd Street East between 2nd and 3rd avenues. The city hoped that the bus mall would result in greater use of the transit system. *Photo LH 6980 courtesy SPL – LHR*

Indian rights in the Canadian law system were the focus of the 1983 annual Indian Justice Conference at the Bessborough Hotel. First Nations people, shown here in opening ceremonies, had been moving into the city from Saskatchewan reserves in increasing numbers since the 1960s. *Photo S-SP 17240-1 courtesy Sask Archives* StarPhoenix *Collection*

A worker repairs the chimney atop the Saskatoon Club at 417 21st Street East in June 1986. In the background are the upper stories of the Bessborough. In 1981, the city had adopted a heritage property policy that encouraged the preservation of high-quality older buildings, especially downtown. *Photo LH 9270 Saskatoon* StarPhoenix, *courtesy SPL – LHR*

Part of downtown viewed from the east side of the river in the summer of 1985. The Ramada Renaissance hotel and condo complex (centre foreground), along with the Sturdy Stone and Saskatoon Square buildings (right centre) transformed the city's skyline. The Meewasin Trail, frequented by joggers, extends along the bank just above the river edge. It was constructed by the Meewasin Valley Authority (MVA), which was established in 1979 to protect and develop the river valley through the city. *Photo LH 8730 courtesy SPL – LHR*

In 1987, teenagers danced and socialized alcohol-free at the Big Apple Pizza A Go Go, located in a former warehouse building at 402 1st Avenue North. Its popularity was short lived, however, and two years later it was replaced by Bleachers, an adult nightclub. *Photo S-SP May 27, 1988 courtesy Sask Archives* StarPhoenix *Collection*

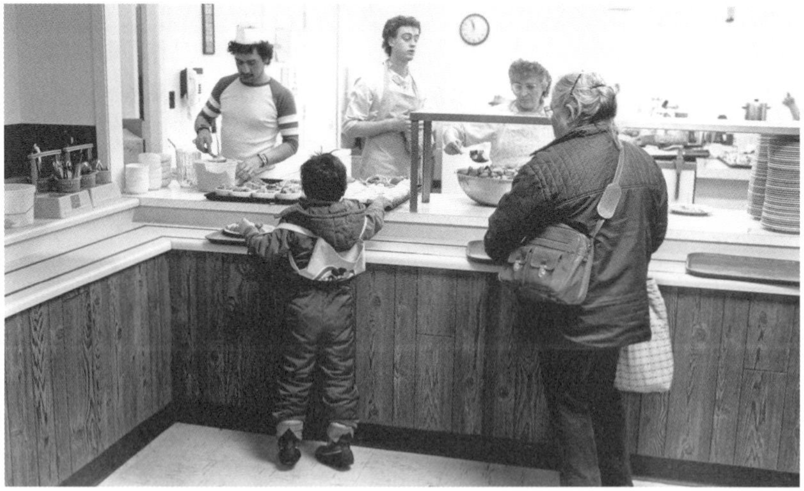

Friendship Inn was established on 20th Street West in 1969 to provide free meals and clothing to transient men. By the late 1980s, about a quarter of the meals served were to needy women and children. *Photo S-SP Jan 30, 1988 courtesy Sask Archives* StarPhoenix *Collection*

Stephen Lander "roof sits" on the balcony of the Senator Hotel over the sidewalk on 21st Street East in January 1988 to raise money for the annual United Way appeal. The sign in the window was used to keep track of the money raised. *Photo S-SP 7011-17A courtesy Sask Archives* StarPhoenix *Collection*

In June 1989, protestors demonstrated against the proposed free trade agreement in front of the Bessborough Hotel while Prime Minister Mulroney (right foreground) was in Saskatoon to meet with the provincial government. *Photo S-SP 296A courtesy Sask Archives* StarPhoenix *Collection*

Gary Tisdale entertains adults and children alike during story hour at Pooh Corner in April 1988 in the children's department of the downtown branch of the Saskatoon Public Library. *Photo PH 88-340 courtesy SPL – LHR*

Welders work on the glassed-faced SEDCO Centre at Innovation Place, ca. 1988. A "research park" established just north of the university campus by the Saskatchewan Economic Development Corporation in 1977, Innovation Place would help establish a high-tech research and development sector in Saskatoon. *Photo SSP Jan 29, 1988 15/15A courtesy Sask Archives* StarPhoenix *Collection*

Looking north over the new Saskatchewan Place arena (now Credit Union Centre) northwest of Saskatoon in February 1988. *SP file photo courtesy* StarPhoenix

Skaters enjoying the Meewasin outdoor skating rink in Kiwanis Park beside the Bessborough on a sunny winter afternoon in 1989. The Meewasin Valley Authority (MVA) has provided an outdoor rink each winter since the 1970s, when the rink was located in front of city hall. *SP file photo courtesy* StarPhoenix

An intrepid youth plummets down a steep slide in 1986, part of the Penguin Park water slide complex then on Idywyld Drive North. Cold, wet weather caused financial difficulties for the facility, which eventually closed. The water slides were dismantled in 1993 and finally shipped to Wichita, Kansas. *SP file photo, 20 Aug. 1986, courtesy* StarPhoenix

In May 1988, the red-and-white Shakespeare on the Saskatchewan tent goes up on the river bank near the Mendel Art Gallery for another season of outdoor theatre in Saskatoon. Started in 1985, the troupe presents Shakespearean plays set in non-Elizabethan times: *A Midsummer Night's Dream* on a golf course, or a heavy-metal version of *Richard III. Photo S-SP 6975 -13/13A courtesy Sask Archives* StarPhoenix *Collection*

The Blairmore Ring potash monument in Rotary Park on the east bank of the river in the summer of 1989. It was erected in 1965 to symbolize the growing importance of the potash industry to Saskatoon. In 2001 it was moved to the John G. Diefenbaker International Airport to make way for the reconstruction of the Rotary Peace Plaza. *Photo courtesy Dick Epp*

Runners of all ages participate in an Olympic Day fun run on June 24, 1989 along the streets and parks of downtown Saskatoon. The run was organized by the YMCA to draw attention to the Jeux Canada Games being held in the city that August. *Photo S-SP 350B-15/15A courtesy Sask Archives* StarPhoenix *Collection*

The Duke and Duchess of York examine the scale model of the bronze sculpture created by local artist Bill Epp to commemorate the 1989 Jeux Canada Games during their visit to Saskatoon in July 1989. The completed piece is one of many of Epp's works that grace the streets and parks of Saskatoon. *Photo courtesy Dick Epp*

In June 1989, the Saskatchewan women's sweep team carry their racing shell to the new canoe clubhouse built on the river bank in Victoria Park. River-based competitions were located there during the Jeux Canada Games, held in Saskatoon later that summer. *Photo S-SP 358B-15/15A courtesy Sask Archives* StarPhoenix *Collection*

Cyprian Enweani, a local athlete and a member of the Canadian Olympic team at Seoul in 1988, lit the flame at Griffiths Stadium during opening ceremonies of the Jeux Canada Games in Saskatoon in 1989. The largest event held in Saskatoon to date, the games were a success in part because of the record number of volunteers who helped run them. *Photo courtesy Dick Epp*

In December 1989, hundreds of people crowded the annual Sundog Handcraft Faire at the Field House, where local artisans marketed their wares. Sundog begun in 1974, reflecting the growing popularity of handcrafting in Saskatoon. *Photo S-SP 7906-11A courtesy Sask Archives* StarPhoenix *Collection*

Rick Folk made his fourteenth consecutive appearance at the Classic bonspiel in December 1989. This bonspiel, which matches local teams with some of the best curlers in the country, has been held at the Nutana Curling Club each winter since 1974. Folk brought Saskatoon international attention in 1980 when he skipped his locally based team to the Canadian Brier championship, then went on to capture the Silver Broom, the world curling championship. *Photo S-SP 512 E-4/4A courtesy Sask Archives* StarPhoenix *Collection*

Chapter Eleven
1990-1999

Saskatoon in the 1990s continued to be plagued by the disagreeable economic baggage it had inherited from the decade before. Unemployment rates continued to be high, contributing to a growing westward migration, particularly of younger people. Trouble in the provincial farm economy coupled with austerity programs by a provincial government desperate to erase a huge budget deficit made things worse. The number of low-income households in Saskatoon rose steadily throughout the 1990s, as did the reliance on food banks and other social safety nets.

Local businesses suffered too. In 1998, both Flexi-Coil and Cameco experienced huge layoffs, as did the Saskatchewan Economic Development Corporation (SEDCO). Canamino, a high-tech oat processing plant located at Innovation Place, was forced into bankruptcy just a few years after its well-publicized debut, and Atomic Energy of Canada (housed in the splendidly retrofitted former Modern Press building on 2nd Avenue) folded as well. Local media outlets were also gutted. Massive layoffs wracked the *StarPhoenix* after it was acquired by the multinational Hollinger Corporation in 1992. The short-lived *Saskatoon Free Press* folded in 1999.

Opposite page: Looking down from the third-floor concourse of the new College of Agriculture building at its official opening in October 1991. This soaring glass edifice was the major addition to the university campus in the 1990s. *Photo S-SP 2866 A-17A courtesy Sask Archives* StarPhoenix *Collection*

The tall pre-cast concrete CIBC building (right) and the glass-faced Scotia Centre and Scotiabank (left) dominated 2nd Avenue in 1990. The overhead walkway that linked the Hudson Bay department store at 23rd Street with its parkade was removed and the parkade demolished in the spring of 2004. *Photo S-SP 1457C-8 courtesy Sask Archives* StarPhoenix *Collection*

CTV suffered layoffs, and the CBC's Saskatoon facilities were drastically downsized in 1990 when programming was centralized in Regina.

Labour unrest and tough economic times go hand in hand. Strikes during the 1990s included workers at the Saskatchewan Wheat Pool, school teachers, civic workers, and the Saskatchewan Union of Nurses.

Despite an overall drop in new construction during the 1990s, some formidable projects were undertaken, including the $117 million Saskatoon City Hospital building, the controversial twelve-storey Broadway Square condominium, which towered over Five Corners, and the spectacular new College of Agriculture building on campus. In 1998, the Bessborough Hotel underwent a major renovation, sprucing up the guest rooms and public areas. In 1999, funding was announced for "Canada's largest-ever science project," the $174 million Canadian Light Source synchrotron at the University of Saskatchewan. It was completed in 2004.

The retail landscape in Saskatoon changed during the 1990s as huge "big box" stores became more common and smaller outlets like Kresge's and Woolworths began to disappear. The giant national retailer Eaton's faltered and failed in 1999 after more than seventy years as one of Saskatoon's premier department stores. The Hudson's Bay Company abandoned its landmark premises at 23rd Street and 2nd Avenue to move into the former Eaton's premises in Midtown Plaza.

All was not total gloom, of course. The biotech research industry burgeoned in the nineties, causing a building boom at Innovation Place north of the university campus. In 1995, the giant food corporation Cargill announced plans to build a new $53.6 million canola-crushing plant near Saskatoon. AgrEvo, a German company, established its North American office for oilseed and cereals biotechnology in Saskatoon. The Potash Corporation of Saskatchewan – headquartered in Saskatoon – bought two jumbo American phosphate producers and doubled its production capacity, and the Federation of Saskatchewan Indian Nations opened the First Nations Bank in the city.

One project that didn't get off the ground in the 1990s was an $80 million casino, trade and convention centre development proposed for Saskatoon's south downtown area. The casino became the focus of a huge grassroots lobbying effort which forced a plebiscite on the issue in the 1994 municipal election, where it was rejected by voters by a four-to-one margin.

The 1990s saw much-needed work undertaken on the city's infrastructure, including new interchanges on Circle Drive and repairs to the University Bridge. One unanticipated alteration in the civic landscape was the partial destruction of Rotary Park, caused by the slumping of the river bank near the Broadway Bridge.

Saskatoon continued to grow. In 1996, the population was reported to have passed the 200,000 mark. But the average age was increasing as post-war baby boomers entered their thirties and forties and young people continued to be lured away by the bright lights of Calgary, Edmonton, and Vancouver. Newcomers to the city were mostly from rural Saskatchewan, as usual, but immigrants from abroad – primarily Asia, southern and eastern Europe, and the Middle East – added to the city's cultural diversity. A wide array of ethnic restaurants added spice to city diets, reflecting the changing ethnic composition of the populace. Half of all immigrants to Saskatchewan settled in Saskatoon. The city's Aboriginal population was also growing, and in 1998 was said to be among the largest in Canada.

In 1992, the main entrance of the Midtown Plaza was rebuilt to resemble the façade of the Canadian Northern Railway station that had stood on that site in 1910. *Photo PH 92259-8 by Bette Sadoway, courtesy SPL – LHR*

Although not comparable to the out-of-control housing markets in places like Toronto and Vancouver, house prices in Saskatoon were also surging by the end of the decade. The popularity of condominiums and other multiple-unit dwellings was also growing. New townhouses and highrise apartment-style condominium complexes began to go up across the city. Rental accommodations were affected as many existing apartment buildings were converted to condominiums, particularly in older neighbourhoods close to downtown. Perhaps not coincidentally, new house construction during the 1990s was significantly lower than in previous decades, with most new development on the east side in Silverspring, Arbor Creek, and Briarwood.

On summer Saturday mornings, the Farmers' Market in front of the downtown library was the place to buy fresh, locally grown produce, homemade food products, and crafts. Socializing was an added draw. In winter, the market moved into the Sturdy Stone Centre mall. *Photo S-SP 1551 F6 courtesy Sask Archives* StarPhoenix *Collection*

Downtown, a new seniors' tower went up on the site of the old Saskatoon Arena on 19th Street. An attempt was made to convert the former A. L. Cole power station on the river bank at Avenue B into an upscale apartment or condominium complex. This fell through, as did the other uses proposed for the building, including an engineering museum and IMAX theatre, a community recreation centre, a cultural centre, and a farmers' market. Despite a great deal of public interest, the associated repair and clean-up costs were far too great, and the building was torn down in 1996.

As the size of Saskatoon's Aboriginal community increased so too did the need for services tailored specifically to its needs. On the recommendations of its Race Relations Committee, the City of Saskatoon hired a Race Relations Coordinator in 1991 to explore ways to minimize racial tension and promote racial harmony within the city. In 1994, the Saskatchewan Indian Federated College (now the First Nations University of Canada) moved into the former Wilson School in City Park. Programs for Aboriginal students were also established at the University of Saskatchewan. North of the city, the Wanuskewin Heritage Park opened in 1992 to act as an historical and interpretive centre for northern plains Aboriginal cultures.

The 1990s was a boisterous decade for the Saskatoon arts and cultural scene. Local authors, artists, photographers, and musicians made waves both here and elsewhere. The Farmers'

In the fall of 1991, the cast of the Saskatoon Soaps announced the opening of a new season from atop the marquee of the Broadway Theatre. Held on Friday nights since the mid-1980s, this madcap improvisational show satirized current issues in the city. The players included James O'Shea, Tom Rooney, Alphonse Gaudet, Jeff Rogstad, Ralph Blankenagel, Elizabeth McRobbie, Rick Gorrie, Brad Grass, and Patricia Drake, many of whom have gone on to careers in theatre or broadcasting. *Photo S-SP 2807A-29 courtesy Sask Archive* StarPhoenix *Collection*

Market moved indoors to the Sturdy Stone Building for the winter but continued its summer location in front of city hall. Former Saskatonian Joni Mitchell received the Governor General's Performing Arts Award and was inducted into the Rock and Roll Hall of Fame in 1996. The large seating capacity of Saskatchewan Place (now the Credit Union Centre) made Saskatoon a potential tour date for even the most popular of performing artists. Canadian and international celebrities such as Bruce Cockburn, Bryan Adams, Rod Stewart, Bob Dylan, and AC/DC all performed in Sask Place during the nineties.

Events such as the Fringe Festival – a celebration of alternative and avant-garde theatre, dance, and musical performance held on Broadway Avenue each August – the River Roar power-boat races, Chinese dragon-boat races, and the popular Taste of Saskatchewan food festival helped round out the summer's schedule of diversions in the 1990s.

In the sporting world, the U of S Huskies won the Vanier Cup three times during the 1990s, while Catriona LeMay Doan brought glory to her hometown with gold medals for speed-skating at the 1998 Winter Olympics.

During the 1990s, Saskatoon and the world entered the Information Age as the price and complexity of home computers came down to the point where they were practical for the average consumer. Sales took off, aided by the immense popularity of the internet. By the end of the decade, half of Saskatoon's homes had a computer, most with an internet connection.

As the decade drew to a close, incomes in Saskatoon were rising and the economy was rebounding. But as the year 2000 approached, so too did a new threat, the dreaded "Y2K" computer bug, which, it was feared, would cause a widespread technological meltdown. Watching as their clocks ticked closer to midnight on the last day of 1999, the people of Saskatoon could not help but feel a certain apprehension as to what the future might hold.

Looking southwest from Maxwell Street on the west side of the city as a funnel cloud passes to the south at about 4 p.m. on June 27, 1990. Tall buildings downtown were evacuated when a tornado warning was received from the airport weather station. The tornado caused considerable damage to crops where it touched down in the Vanscoy area. *Photo PH 95-73 by Roger Kane, courtesy SPL – LHR*

Wanuskewin, a national heritage site north of Saskatoon, was a fitting place for the official signing of a land entitlement agreement between the Federation of Saskatchewan Indian Nations (FSIN) and the governments of Canada and Saskatchewan in September 1992. Prime Minister Brian Mulroney, FSIN Chief Roland Crowe, and Premier Roy Romanow signed on behalf of their respective constituencies. *Photo S-SP 3644A-20A courtesy Sask Archives* StarPhoenix *Collection*

Line dancers attempt to set a new indoor record in the corridors of Market Mall in February 1993. Line dancing attracted a following beyond the usual country music fans in the early 1990s. *Photo S-SP 3917L-7A courtesy Sask Archives* StarPhoenix *Collection*

Looking northward in the spring of 1993 from the boom of a construction crane being used to build Clinkskill Manor seniors' high rise on 19th Street East on the site of the Saskatoon Arena, which was demolished in 1989. In the middle is Block 146, most of which is now under development. *Photo S-SP 4055A 2A/3 courtesy Sask Archives* StarPhoenix *Collection*

One of the plans for the redevelopment of the south downtown prepared by consultants during the 1990s. This one, presented in 1993, proposed the reuse of the former A. L. Cole power plant (background) as a "River Centre." An earlier attempt by private entrepreneurs to convert the A. L. Cole plant into residential condominiums had failed. The structure, except for the pump house (left middle), was demolished in 1996. *SP file photo courtesy* StarPhoenix

In 1994, the Riversdale Business Improvement District commissioned artist Jaing Wan to paint this colourful dragon mural on the wall of A.J.'s video store at 20th Street West and Avenue D. It is one of several buildings in Riversdale painted to celebrate the cultural mix of the area. *Photo S-SP 5049B-13 courtesy Sask Archives* StarPhoenix *Collection*

City workers gather on the city hall grounds for a Labour Day rally during a 1994 city-wide municipal strike that lasted ten weeks. This walkout demonstrated how important civic services such as garbage disposal, transit, and libraries are to everyday life in Saskatoon. *SP file photo courtesy* StarPhoenix

Catriona LeMay Doan was greeted with much fanfare on her return to Saskatoon in May 1998, in celebration of the gold medals she won in speed skating at the Winter Olympics in Nagano, Japan. *SP file photo, 7 May 1998, courtesy* StarPhoenix

Young dancers at the Karpaty Ukrainian Pavilion at Folkfest in August 1990. Since its beginning in the 1980s, Folkfest has attracted thousands to sample the cuisine, costumes, and dance in twenty-some ethnic pavilions each summer. *SP file photo, 31 Aug. 1996, courtesy* StarPhoenix

Jazz Festival fans relax in the Bessborough Gardens in July 1993. Since 1987, the annual summer festival has brought jazz, world music, and blues bands from all over North America to perform in the city. *SP file photo, 4 July 1993, courtesy Sask Archives* StarPhoenix *Collection*

Since the late 1980s, children have flocked to Kiwanis Park on the west river bank each spring for several days of storytelling, music, theatre, dance, face-painting, and clowns at the Northern Saskatchewan International Children's Festival. *SP file photo courtesy* StarPhoenix

Saskatoon writers and their spouses gather for a repast in 1998: (l to r) Jill Robinson, Stephen Ross Smith, Rod MacPherson, Jeannie MacPherson, Will Rogers, John Livingstone Clark, David Carpenter (seated), and Darlene Clark (now Kutzel). *Photo 99-35-1 by Joy Von Tiedemann, courtesy* SPL – LHR

Starting in 1998, dragon boat races have been a popular event each spring. Teams representing various businesses and institutions compete in decorated boats on the river. *Photo S-SP 7011E-27A courtesy Sask Archives* StarPhoenix *Collection*

Marchers protesting an anti-gay ad carried in the *StarPhoenix* in July 1997. Gay men and women in Saskatoon have been "coming out" in increasing numbers since the high-profile Doug Wilson case at the university in the mid-1970s. *SP file photo, 3 July 1997, courtesy* StarPhoenix

A young "crowd surfer" skims above the mosh pit at a concert at Saskatchewan Place (now Credit Union Centre) in 1998. A crowd of 15,000 teenagers and twenty-somethings rocked to the sounds of thirteen bands at Edgefest, a nine-hour outdoor concert. *SP file photo, 6 July 1998, courtesy* StarPhoenix

A crew processes used beverage containers at the Sarcan outlet at the Churchill Shopping Centre in November 1995. The rise of the environmental movement, sparked partly by the energy crisis of the 1970s and dwindling nonrenewable resources, resulted in recycling programs across Canada to prolong the useful life of metals, glass, and plastics. *SP file photo, 23 Nov. 1995, courtesy* StarPhoenix

The ethnic and religious mosaic in Saskatoon had dramatically altered by the 1990s, as reflected in this 1995 scene. Here Gurbachan Basran looks on while Surjut Lalli examines holy writings in the Sikh temple. *SP file photo, 19 Oct. 1995, courtesy* StarPhoenix

The 1999 CKOM-FM 102 Cruise Night brought about seven hundred vintage cars, trucks, and motorcycles on to the city's streets. Annual car shows such as this have been a popular attraction in Saskatoon for many years. *Photo S-SP 7056A 9A/10 courtesy Sask Archives* StarPhoenix *Collection*

Chapter Twelve

THE TWENTY-FIRST CENTURY

The best news of the first few minutes of the year 2000 was that all the feverish work that had gone into preparing for the "Y2K" computer bug had paid off. The world's machines did not suddenly grind to a halt as their internal clocks – accustomed to counting the years in two digits only – suddenly thought that it was the year 1900. Chaos did not reign, airplanes did not fall, and civilization survived. It was a measure of how ubiquitous the computer had become that it was ever an issue at all.

By 2003 almost 70 per cent of Canadian homes had a computer in them. Sophisticated video game systems, wireless cellular telephones, and a vast array of other high-tech gadgets also invaded the consumer market at this time, riding on the coattails of the home computer's popularity. Like the radio in the 1920s, the computer and all the other electronic wizardry it helped to spawn caused a revolution in the way that people worked, played, and communicated.

As usual, Saskatoon felt the effects of international economic and political tensions. The most notable of these may have been the terrorist attacks on the United States in September 2001 and that country's response to them. But the

---

Opposite page: View from the roof as a circle of Aboriginal drummers and dancers celebrated the official reopening of Joe Duquette High School on Broadway Avenue in the fall of 2000. Formerly known as the Native Survival School, the name honours the first elder there, a Federation of Saskatchewan Indian Nations senator who died in 1988. *SP photo by Gord Waldner, 30 Sept. 2000, courtesy* StarPhoenix

A work crew tears down the temporary bleachers at the south end of Saskatchewan Place (Credit Union Centre) following the windup of the 2000 Brier curling championship. The many volunteers were credited with making this national event a success and for Saskatoon being chosen as the site of the Brier again in 2004. *SP photo by Gordon Waldner, 13 Mar. 2000, courtesy* StarPhoenix

discovery in 2003 of a Canadian cow suffering from the colourfully named Mad Cow Disease led to the immediate closing of the American (and other) borders to Canadian cattle and had devastating consequences for area cattle producers. Farmers also suffered from serious drought conditions in the first half of the decade, with 2001 being Saskatoon's driest year in a century. While the city's economic well-being no longer depended solely on the health of the farm economy, what affected the farmers continued to affect Saskatoon.

Despite the troubled agricultural sector, Saskatoon grew and prospered during the first half of the first decade of the twenty-first century. The "big box" trend that had begun here in the 1990s continued as work began on the Preston Crossing retail development in the spring of 2002. The Canadian Light Source (CLS) synchrotron project at the University of Saskatchewan was completed in the fall of 2004. The size of a football field, and considered to be one of the most technologically advanced synchrotrons in the world, the CLS may be the most important piece of new construction to occur in Saskatoon this decade.

In 2000, seventy years of retail history came to an end when the Army and Navy Department Store (a building originally occupied by Eaton's) at the corner of 3rd Avenue and 21st Street downtown closed for good. The building was converted into office space for the Saskatoon Public School Board. Controversy swirled around the fate of the former school board offices in the Gathercole Building (the old Saskatoon Technical Collegiate on the river bank in Saskatoon's south downtown area) between those who wished to see it reused and those who wished to tear it down. It was finally demolished in the summer of 2004 to make way for River Landing, a mix of public and private development stretching along the river bank from the Victoria Avenue Traffic Bridge west into the old A.L. Cole site.

Aboriginal and race relations continued to be important issues in Saskatoon during the first decade of the new century. In 2001, Saskatoon's Aboriginal population stood at just over 20,000, almost double what it had been a decade before and more than four times what it had been in 1981. This trend is expected to continue. Provincial population projections suggest that by 2050 between one-third and one-half of Saskatchewan's population will be Aboriginal.

Environmental initiatives also became increasingly important during this time. Public dialogue about improved bicycle routes, better public transit, alternative energy sources, composting, and recycling all pointed to a city more concerned with the future of the natural environment than ever before. The City of Saskatoon began exploring "green" alternatives, purchasing canola-fuelled "bio-buses," setting up large-scale composting and recycling projects, and establishing an environmental protection branch. A further attempt to "clear the air" occurred in 2004 when city council passed a very controversial smoking bylaw which banned smoking in all indoor public places and private clubs.

Child-care workers and their charges parade from Kinsmen Park to city hall to celebrate Child-Care Week in the spring of 2000. Requests for government-assisted child-care programs and daycare centres, particularly since the 1970s, increased as more women entered the work force. *SP photo by Gordon Waldner, 19 May 2000, courtesy* StarPhoenix

Other important projects included the official opening of the $23.5 million Circle Drive and 22nd Street Interchange in 2002 (completed on time and under budget) and the Meewasin Valley Authority's impressive River Walk development along the west bank of the river just below the 33rd Street weir.

In the fall of 2005 the Victoria Avenue Traffic Bridge was closed following an engineering report warning that it was in a state of advanced deterioration. Corrosion had taken a heavy toll on the historic structure's steel frame. The civic administration was

Cyclists huff and puff up the Broadway Bridge in support of the environment on World Car-Free Day in September 2000. Others took the bus, skated, walked, or jogged. *SP photo by Richard Marjan, 22 Sept. 2000, courtesy* StarPhoenix

forced to decide whether to attempt to repair it, replace it with a replica, or replace it with a modern concrete bridge. The suggestion that it be converted into a bicycle and pedestrian crossing was dismissed, as the bridge would continue to deteriorate until it was unable to support even its own weight.

It was a cruel irony that on the eve of Saskatoon's centennial year the bridge that had played such a large role in its incorporation seemed doomed to fall to the wrecker's ball.

As of December 2005, the bridge is closed and undergoing further study. Public opinion seems to be split between those who demand it be saved and those who call for it to be destroyed. Whatever happens, the city cannot afford to lose a downtown river crossing, and it seems likely that there will continue to be a bridge of some sort in that spot in the future.

The first decade of the twenty-first century contains three important centennials: the province's in 2005; the city's in 2006, and the university's in 2007. While it is important during events like these to re-examine our past and remember all the things that got us to where we are now, it is equally important to look ahead. In Saskatoon, in 2006, the past and the future will meet.

It would be useless to try and paint a picture of the Saskatoon of the future save with the very broadest of brushes. A brief reading of newspaper and magazine articles from the 1950s and 1960s predicting life in the year 2000 is suffi-

The new air control tower under construction at the John G. Diefenbaker International Airport in October 2000. This was the beginning of a major expansion of the airport after its operation was turned over to the Saskatoon Airport Authority in 1999. *SP photo by Gordon Waldner, 17 Oct. 2000, courtesy* StarPhoenix cient to show that future trends in technology, popular culture, fad, and fashion are nearly impossible to foretell with any accuracy. Yet in some areas we can be reasonably certain what the future will hold (barring any unforeseen catastrophe, of course), particularly regarding population growth and urban development.

In 1999, the city unveiled the Saskatoon Downtown Plan, which set up a system of tax incentives aimed at encouraging residential development in the city's downtown, including new apartment construction and the renovation of existing commercial and warehouse buildings to allow for residential and mixed residential/commercial use. The goal of the plan is for the residential population of downtown to double (to 10,000) by 2024. A planned extension of 25th Street to Idylwyld Drive, relocation of the city yards out of the warehouse district, and other changes to the area are also expected to help spur residential growth downtown.

By 2011, Saskatoon is expected to have a population of 237,000 – double the population of a half-century earlier and ten times the population in 1911. But Saskatoon's city planners are already preparing for a city of 400,000. Major development is slated to take place south of Circle Drive (between Clarence Avenue and Highway 11); in the city's southeastern tip; northeast of the Forestry Farm and the present-day Silverspring area; and in a large block of land west of the city centred along 22nd Street.

Interestingly, this far-distant west sector development will include areas that were surveyed, subdivided, and sold (but never built on) nearly a century ago, at the height of Saskatoon's great land boom. It is there that our future will finally catch up to our past: on a piece of bald prairie once suitable only to be unloaded on the gullible for 5 per cent down and ten dollars a month and, finally, to be home to the thousands of new citizens that the dreamers of old envisaged for it.

Premier Lorne Calvert took part in the official unveiling of the name of the White Buffalo Lodge at 602 20th Street West in September 2001. According to tradition, the white buffalo symbolizes new beginnings and a return to healing and balance. The lodge offers health and elder services, as well as recreation, sports, and cultural programs. *SP photo by Greg Pender, 2 Sept. 2001, courtesy* StarPhoenix

Three maids a-milking was one display in the second annual Enchanted Forest light show sponsored by the Saskatchewan Indian Gaming Authority (SIGA) at the Forestry Farm in January 2000. The proceeds from this annual winter show are split by the Saskatoon City Hospital Foundation and the Saskatoon Zoo Foundation. *SP photo, 15 Jan. 2000, courtesy* StarPhoenix

For decades, Saskatonians have flocked to the Wiggins Avenue home of former teacher Robert Hinitt, to see his annual front-yard Christmas display. In December 2001, the theme was Charlotte's Web, inspired by a children's book. The highlight was a four-metre moving ferris wheel carrying handmade human figures, pigs, spiders, and rats. *SP photo, 28 Dec. 2001, courtesy* StarPhoenix

The Saskatoon City Police participated in a tribute held on September 18, 2001, on the city hall grounds for emergency workers killed in the attack on the World Trade Centre in New York a week earlier. *SP photo by Greg Pender, 18 Sept. 2001, courtesy* StarPhoenix

A crowd gathered on Broadway Avenue to watch street acts at the Fringe Festival in August 2002. The first festival of alternative theatre, live music, and street performances in Saskatoon was held during Festival Saskatoon, part of the Jeux Canada Games celebrations in 1989. Fringe festivals have been held annually since, migrating from the Broadway area to south downtown, to the downtown warehouse area, and finally back to Broadway. *SP photo, 11 Aug. 2002, courtesy* StarPhoenix

"C-Pig Fly," sponsored by SREDA and Tourism Saskatoon, was unveiled in May 2002 before being put on display on Airport Drive. It was one of eighteen whimsically decorated hogs located about the city that summer before being auctioned off as part of the Saskatoon Abilities Council's "Pigs in the City" fundraiser. These porkers drew considerable attention, particularly when "Miss Sowskatoon" surreptitiously ended up on the mayor's lawn. *SP photo, 7 May 2002, courtesy* StarPhoenix

Saskatoon Public Library workers picket in front of the Frances Morrison Branch on 23rd Street East in September 2002. They had gone on strike to back their demand for pay equity with other civic employees doing similar work. *SP photo, 25 Sept. 2002, courtesy* StarPhoenix

Renowned Aboriginal actor Gordon Tootoosis gallops past the Wanuskewin Interpretive Centre during filming of the historic movie Big Bear in 1998. StarPhoenix *file photo*

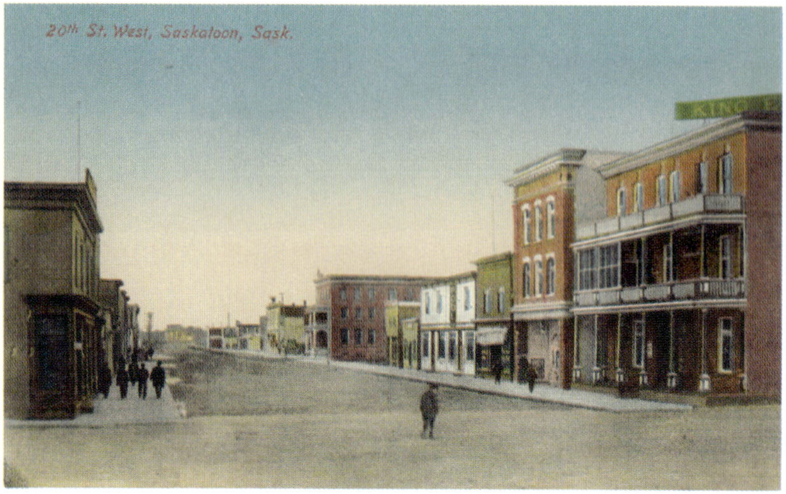

The King Edward Hotel features prominently at right in this view of 20th Street West in Riversdale, before 1913. *Photo LH 4120, courtesy Saskatoon Public Library Local History Room*

21st Street East, looking west toward the former CNR station, probably in the 1950s. In the distance are the former CNR Station and rail yards. *Photo PH 93-166-1, courtesy Saskatoon Public Library Local History Room*

Some prominent buildings in this vintage view of Broadway Avenue (looking north) still remain: the Sommerfeld Block, the "Royal Bank Building" (no longer a bank), and the Eaton Block at right, and two buildings once owned by druggist C.H. Stewart at left. *Photo PH 88-88, courtesy Saskatoon Public Library Local History Room*

3rd Avenue South, looking north. Most of these buildings have survived, and some have even been refurbished, including the Avenue Building and the Eaton's building on the right. The Birk's building (in the distance) and the Flanagan Hotel at left (now the Senator) are still being used as a store and a hotel, respectively. *Photo PH 95-78-14, courtesy Saskatoon Public Library Local History Room*

The College Building (also known as the Administration Building) on the University of Saskatchewan campus reopened to much fanfare in 2005, after extensive – and expensive – restorations. © *Pro-stock Images, Saskatoon*

The 2000 Brier curling championships attracted vast crowds to the Saskatchewan Place arena, renamed Credit Union Centre in 2003. StarPhoenix *file photo*

The Canadian Light Source Synchrotron, located at the University of Saskatchewan campus, was opened October 22nd, 2004, reinforcing Saskatoon's status as a science and technology centre. *Photo courtesy Canadian Light Source Inc., U of S*

Former Governor General Ramon (Ray) Hnatyshyn admires a likeness of himself at the public unveiling of the monument in Kiwanis Park, in September 1992. Comissioned by the Ukranian Canadian Congress, the sculpture was created by Bill Epp. StarPhoenix *file photo*

Two-year-old Brynn Wuttunee dances with her mother Melissa and other dancers during the grand entry of a Federation of Saskatchewan Indian Nations powwow at Credit Union Centre. StarPhoenix *file photo*

Thousands of ecstatic fans packed the Credit Union Centre to watch Theresa Sokyrka on the big screen in the final of the television show *Canadian Idol* show in Sept. 2004. Though she finished as runner-up, Theresa was still Saskatoon's darling in the nationally televised singing competition. Star-Phoenix *file photo*

Saskatchewan fiddler John Arcand greets the Queen at the Lieutenant Governor's Centennial Gala at Credit Union Centre in May, 2005. StarPhoenix *file photo*

Crowds estimated at up to 70,000 people celebrated the province's centenary at Diefenbaker Park in September 2005. The celebration featured ten hours of "heritage games," live music and entertainment, climaxed by a spectacular "pyro-musical" fireworks display. StarPhoenix *file photo*

Completion of construction of the new Saskatoon City Hospital was celebrated in August, 1993. In a climate of severe economic constraints, the impressive state-of-the-art building, with a price tag of $117 million, was an improbable achievement. It officially opened that October. StarPhoenix *file photo*

This contemporary vista of downtown Saskatoon at night bears no resemblance to that of the newborn city in 1906. © *Pro-stock Images, Saskatoon*

The final total raised by the thirty-sixth annual Kinsmen Telemiracle was broadcast on CFQC-TV from the stage of the Centennial Auditorium in March 2003. This province-wide telethon, held in Saskatoon every second year (alternating with Regina), had raised about $55 million by 2003 to help the handicapped in Saskatchewan. *SP photo, 2 Mar. 2002, courtesy* StarPhoenix

Powerboats race under the Victoria Avenue Traffic Bridge in July 2003 during River Roar, an international Grand Prix Formula competition hosted in Saskatoon most summers since 1992. Spectators could choose from a wide range of foods and refreshments at A Taste of Saskatchewan, a food court set up by local restaurants in a tent city (right centre) in Friendship Park. *Photo by Doug Porteous, courtesy MVA*

Looking southwest in August 2003 at some "big box" stores in the first phase of the Preston Crossing shopping centre, located on land leased from the university in the northeast of the city. *SP photo by Richard Marjan, 29 Aug. 2003, courtesy* StarPhoenix

The Saskatoon Hilltops celebrated their third consecutive national junior football championship on November 10, 2003. They had just defeated the Victoria Rebels in the Canadian Bowl championship game played in Chilliwack, BC. *SP photo, 10 Nov. 2003, courtesy* StarPhoenix

Sue Barrett (left) and Donna Baldwin hosted a Saskatoon Heritage Society reception on August 25, 2002, to celebrate the opening of the Marr Garden in the back yard of the Marr Residence at 326 Main Street. The oldest house still on its original site, the Marr Residence is one of a number of municipal heritage properties designated in Saskatoon. *SP photo, 25 Aug. 2002, courtesy* StarPhoenix

Despite the protests of heritage groups, city council voted to have the Gathercole Centre torn down in 2004 to make way for a planned "River Landing" development in the south downtown. Here, workers carefully disassemble the southeast entrance so it might be incorporated into future development on the site. *Photo courtesy MVA*

The official opening of the Lions' Skateboard Park in Victoria Park on September 29, 2003. Another skateboard park was constructed next to the Lakewood Civic Centre on the south-east side of the city in 2004. *SP photo, 29 Sept. 2003, courtesy* StarPhoenix

The 2003 Festival of Trees, held in Boomtown at the Western Development Museum. This annual event is sponsored by the Saskatoon City Hospital Foundation, with proceeds going to the purchase of emergency medical equipment. *Photo by the Saskatoon Camera Club, courtesy Saskatoon City Hospital Foundation*

Since Saskatoon's earliest days, theatre has been a vibrant ingredient in local culture. Here, the Summer Players pose on stage in Castle Theatre at Aden Bowman Collegiate to promote their production of the musical production *West Side Story* in June 2004. *SP photo by Gordon Waldner, 16 June 2004, courtesy* StarPhoenix

More than 3,500 visitors toured the Canadian Light Source synchrotron on the university campus during an open house in November 2004. *SP photo, 1 Nov. 2004, courtesy* StarPhoenix

Theresa Sokyrka, a finalist in the CTV musical talent show *Canadian Idol,* returned to her hometown for several public appearances in September 2004. She won strong support from Saskatonians young and old and served as the province's Youth Ambassador during the provincial centennial celebrations in 2005. *SP photo, 5 Sept. 2004, courtesy* StarPhoenix

By the fall of 2005, the Riverfront Park (financed by the MVA) was taking shape. It is part of the city's "River Landing" development that is expected to follow directly (on both sides of the Senator Buckwold Bridge) on the city-owned land encompassed by 19th Street. The need for a major restoration or replacement of the Victoria Bridge, which has served this part of the city since 1907, will affect the redevelopment of the south downtown in the years to come. *SP photo by Richard Marjan, 17 Oct. 2005, courtesy* StarPhoenix

On June 20, 2005, a crowd gathered on the Realty Executives Boardwalk to watch as the rising river approached the height of the weir. This boardwalk, extending along the river from the Prince of Wales Promenade (officially opened in September 2001) is part of the ongoing improvement of the Meewasin Trail. *Photo by Rick Stark, courtesy Realty Executives Saskatoon*

Index

About the Authors

PHOTO: RUTH MILLAR

PHOTO: RUTH MILLAR

PHOTO: PHIL CELS

Jeff O'Brien is the City of Saskatoon Archivist. A native of Regina, he did his undergraduate work in history at the university there before moving to Vancouver to complete a Masters degree in Archival Studies at UBC. He has lived in Saskatoon since 1995 and is married, with three children, and four cats.

Ruth W. Millar is a journalist and historian who worked for many years as the head of the local history room at the Saskatoon Public Library. Her writing has appeared in such publications such as *Western People, Saskatoon History Review, Saskatchewan History,* and the *StarPhoenix*. Her first book, *Saskatchewan Heroes and Rogues,* was published by Coteau Books in 2004. She has also made frequent appearances on radio and television.

William P. Delainey is a retired history teacher in the Saskatoon Public School system who works at the local history room of the Saskatoon Public Library. He has received recognition from the City of Saskatoon for his contributions to local history and community planning over the last thirty years. He has published a number of articles on Saskatoon, and is the co-author of *Saskatoon: A Century in Pictures*, with William A.S. Sarjeant and John D. Duerkop.